San Francisco Seafood

SAVORY RECIPES FROM EVERYBODY'S FAVORITE SEAFOOD CITY

Michele Anna Jordan

TEN SPEED PRESS

BERKELEY/TORONTO

Ten Speed Press
P.O. Box 7123
Berkeley, California 94707
www.tenspeed.com

Distributed in Australia by Simon and Schuster Australia, in Canada by Ten Speed Press Canada, in New Zealand by Southern Publishers Group, in South Africa by Real Books, in Southeast Asia by Berkeley Books, and in the United Kingdom and Europe by Airlift Book Company.

Project Editor: Clancy Drake
Text by Michele Anna Jordan
Cover and interior design by Big Fish
Composition by Poulson Gluck Design
Illustrations by Stephanie Heald

Special thanks to Amy Rennert

Library of Congress Cataloging-in-Publication Data
Jordan, Michele Anna
    San Francisco seafood : savory recipes from everybody's favorite seafood city / Michele
    Anna Jordan.
        p. cm.
    Includes index.
    ISBN 1-58008-216-5
    1. Cookery (Seafood) 2. Cookery—California—San Francisco. I. Title

    TX747 .J674 2000
    641.6'92—dc21

                                                                00-057771

First printing, 2000
Printed in the United States of America

1 2 3 4 5 6 7 8 9 10 — 04 03 02 01 00

For Miss Olive, my feline familiar,
who always knows when I've got sand dabs

For the men and women who fish the California coast

And with special thanks to all the restaurants and chefs
for their generous contributions to this book

Also by Michele Anna Jordan

Pasta
The New Cook's Tour of Sonoma
Salt & Pepper
California Home Cooking
Polenta
Pasta with Sauces
Ravioli & Lasagne
The Good Cook's Book of Days: A Food Lover's Journal
The Good Cook's Book of Tomatoes
The Good Cook's Book of Mustard
The Good Cook's Book of Oil & Vinegar
A Cook's Tour of Sonoma

CONTENTS

Acknowledgments

Countless people contributed to *San Francisco Seafood,* including dozens I have never met. Thanks very much to all of the assistants, publicists, hosts and hostesses, and restaurant managers who served as liaisons between me and the chefs who offered recipes for this book.

And to Mary Karlin, who was project manager during the recipe-gathering phase of the book, thank you so much. I never could have completed this project without Mary's invaluable assistance. She came in at the end, too, to help with the final details, so make that a double thanks.

A big thank-you to Roslyn Layton for coordinating restaurant wine recommendations; and to Bill Traverso, of Traverso's Market in Santa Rosa, thanks again for all the wine suggestions and for clearing up several mysteries along the way.

Amy Rennert, my agent, worked hard to make this project a success and I am deeply indebted to her for her part. Thanks so much, Amy.

Francis Bowles, who is one of the world's great copyeditors and also a dear friend, offered crucial assistance, advice, and encouragement when I most needed it. Carolyn Miller, who copyedited the entire manuscript, did a fine job creating consistency among so many disparate techniques and styles. It was a big job; thanks, Carolyn.

One of the best parts of writing this book was working with Windy Ferges at Ten Speed Press, and Clancy Drake, the book's managing editor. You two are awesome; thank you.

Finally, many thanks to all the chefs who saw *San Francisco Seafood* as a worthy project. The book belongs to all of you.

ABOUT THE RECIPES

Everyone, it seems, thinks they understand life in contemporary restaurant kitchens. We see chefs at work on countless television programs, and cookbooks document life at the professional stove with detailed narratives, elaborate recipes, and dramatic photographs. Among the most coveted dinner reservations are those at chef's tables, tables tucked into corners of kitchens in some of the best restaurants in the nation. Affluent home cooks install professional stoves, wood-burning ovens, and pricey granite counters in their designer kitchens.

Yet none of these things, neither the cooking shows, tell-all books, and dinners in the eye of the storm nor the high BTUs of a Viking range can really convey day-to-day life in a commercial kitchen. I tell you this now not to intimidate you but to encourage you to relax.

Unless you have a skilled staff at your disposal, some of the recipes in this book likely will seem overwhelming. If they do, it's not because you lack skills but because these recipes have been developed by executive chefs who rely on several people to execute a complex dish. There may be two or three people preparing ingredients, another making stocks and sauces, someone in the pantry washing and drying greens, and yet another making condiments. These elements will be taken care of long before the restaurant opens for the day. When it comes time to finish a dish—or, in chef's jargon, plate it—there are line cooks to handle the final presentation on plates and bowls that have been warmed in a low oven or, in the best-equipped restaurants, a special plate-warming box.

An executive chef shapes a restaurant's menu, orders ingredients and examines them when they are delivered, develops dishes and their presentations, and teaches staff members how foods should look and taste. The ultimate responsibility and acclaim belong to the executive chef but there may be a dozen or more employees who make his or her vision a reality. At home, we're on our own. Most of us are responsible for every element in a recipe, from shopping for ingredients to presenting the final dish. *Of course* chefs' recipes often seem unwieldy.

San Francisco Seafood is a departure for me. The other twelve books I have written focus primarily on my own recipes, developed and tested in my modest but oh-so-charming home kitchen. I quit working in restaurants years ago, and I have resisted the temptation to buy a Viking range, for example, because I feel a genuine responsibility to my readers. My recipes work for the home cook. The recipes in this book work, too; they have been tested in my kitchen. Where necessary, I have made adjustments so that a recipe will be more accessible to the nonprofessional cook.

Still, in some recipes there are pricey and perhaps unfamiliar ingredients, stocks that are best when simmered for hours, and techniques that lend themselves to the higher heat of a restaurant stove. At the back of the book are basic recipes for stocks, sauces, and condiments and a discussion of many of the techniques necessary to cook seafood with confidence and skill. As you begin a recipe, see what special techniques are necessary and read about them before you begin. Here, I discuss essential elements that you should understand before you begin any of the recipes in this book.

First of all, find a good source for seafood and make a friend of your fish-monger. If you don't live near a seafood market, find a supermarket with a good butcher and find out what he or she can order for you. Be sure to check your local farmers' market, too; some of the larger ones have a seafood vendor or two.

If you don't understand something—how to get skate wing fillets, for example—ask. Ask when a fish was caught or when it arrived in the store; ask if it has been frozen or if it is farmed or wild. You'll find that over a few short weeks, you will have gained a tremendous amount of knowledge. And you'll have a new friend, too. After a while, you might even be able to get your oysters shucked, a service provided by some but not all markets. When you do, be sure to request that the liquor be reserved. (If you'll be serving raw oysters, you can't have them shucked in advance, of course, but if you're making oyster chowder or oyster loaf, getting someone else to do the shucking is a big help.)

Which Salt? What Pepper?

Most recipes, including those in this book, call for "salt and freshly ground pepper to taste." The proper use of salt as you cook allows flavors to blossom, a fact that the best chefs understand intuitively. If you add salt as you cook, to onions as they sauté, for example, you build layers of flavor so that you need to add very little salt at the end to finish a dish. It is difficult, and often impossible, to achieve a proper balance of flavors merely by adding salt after a dish is cooked.

Recipes that indicate a specific salt such as sel gris, a solar-dried sea salt from the Atlantic coast of France, reflect the chef's preference. Sea salt as a generic term is a bit misleading. It refers to salt that is made with sea-water; it is frequently refined and often identical to table salt. Solar-dried sea salt is not refined. In this book, kosher salt refers to Diamond Crystal brand, a fast-dissolving crystal that many cooks and chefs, myself included, prefer.

Black peppercorns contain volatile oils in their outer mantle that dissipate as soon as the mantle is cracked, so for the fullest flavor, add a few twists of black pepper just before serving a dish. White pepper has fewer volatile oils and a deeper, almost fermented taste that stands up to lengthy cooking.

You shouldn't rely exclusively on your fishmonger. Train your senses to recognize fresh fish and to understand when fish is past its prime. Your sense of smell is your first line of defense, a tool you can employ with your eyes closed. Fish should not smell fishy; it should have a clean, briny aroma. If it doesn't, if you've gotten it home only to have it infuse your kitchen with that overpoweringly fishy odor, take it back. But if you can smell it before you buy it—something that is impossible when fish is sold tightly wrapped in plastic—you'll be ahead of the game.

Fish should look good, too, bright, shiny, and moist. Fish should glisten. In most cases, the eyes should be clear and protruding rather than

Olive & Other Oils

All of the recipes in this book were tested with a mild olive oil unless a different oil is specified. Some chefs called for canola oil, others for generic vegetable oil, some for peanut oil or safflower oil. In all cases where a neutral-tasting oil with a high smoke point was called for, I substituted olive oil and I did so in order to simplify the recipes. Olive oil is, I believe, the best all-purpose oil. Its smoke point, the temperature at which it begins to burn, is comparable to other cooking oils, and studies seem to indicate that it is among the healthiest of all oils.

The production of olive oil also is fairly benign to the environment. Olives have very few natural pests, and so it is fairly easy to grow the trees without pesticides or herbicides. Production is straightforward, too. Many oils, including the popular canola oil, require chemicals such as hexene for extraction, but olive oil needs only to be pressed out of the fruit and separated from the vegetable water squeezed out at the same time to be comestible.

A decade ago, cost was an issue when it came to choosing an olive oil. Today prices have declined substantially. It was once necessary to keep a tin of inexpensive pure olive oil for high-heat cooking, moderately priced extra virgin olive oil for making dressings and sauces, and a pricey extra virgin olive oil for flavoring. Now, extra virgin olive oil is inexpensive enough to be used for everyday cooking. I use Sasso, an Italian import, and American Classics, from a California company, for general cooking and keep a selection of artisan olive oils to use as condiments. The subtle flavors of an oil are altered at 140°, so it is a waste to cook with an oil you value for its unique flavors.

Olive oil, and most other oils, should be stored in a cool cupboard away from heat and light. They should never be stored in the refrigerator because their flavors will be altered at lower temperatures. (Unrefined hazelnut oil and walnut oil, however, are very delicate and must be stored in the refrigerator.) You should use oils within six months of purchasing; three is better for flavorful oils.

sunken. Some bottom fish have cloudy eyes, and you will come to recognize these as you become more familiar with a wide range of seafood.

Your sense of touch is also essential. Pushing a fish or a fillet gently with your fingertips will tell you a lot about a fish; it should be somewhat firm—a characteristic that varies among species and resilient. A mushy texture tells you that a fish has been out of the water for too long, that it is beginning to break down. The very freshest fish, those from the live seafood markets of Chinatown, for example, may be somewhat stiff, an indication that the fish has only recently been killed. A fish cooked at this point is sweeter and more succulent than it would be if cooked several hours or even days after its final breath.

Many seafood recipes, including those in this book, call for fish that is pan-dressed. In most cases, this indicates a fish whose head, fins, and scales have been removed. Smaller fish are almost always sold pan-dressed, and many larger ones are, too. Virtually all fish sold in retail markets have been dressed, which is to say the fish has been cleaned of its entrails, or gutted. Some larger fish such as salmon are cleaned before they ever reach the shore; leaving the guts in place after a fish has died hastens spoilage. Whole salmon and other whole fish may still have their scales; ask, and if you're uncertain how to scale a fish, ask the salesperson to do it for you or to show you how to do it. It is not difficult, but it's a task best learned by watching another do it.

Once you bring a fish home, you should keep it as cold as possible until you cook it. Some vendors recommend keeping your fish directly on ice until you use it, and many will pack a fish with crushed ice. You do not, however, want fish to sit in water, so drain it off as the ice melts. I find that a two-inch hotel pan, as the inserts for chafing dishes are called, is a good storage vessel. Fill one about half full with crushed ice, cover the ice with two layers of plastic wrap, set the fish on top, and cover it with a layer of plastic wrap and a clean tea towel.

To store live oysters, set them in a bowl with their cup sides down and cover them with damp tea towels. Although freshly harvested oysters may keep for several days, it is best to use them immediately because you cannot always know how long they've been out of the water. The same is true for other shellfish. Live crab should be prepared the day it is purchased.

To handle fish comfortably, you'll need an excellent boning knife, one that is sharp and flexible. All knives need a good, sturdy blade, of course. Buy a reputable brand and learn how to sharpen it. And when you make your selection, hold several different knives. How a knife fits into your hand is one of its most important qualities. I prefer Henckels Professional series because their handles fit my palm perfectly. My hand never gets tired when I use these knives, as always happens with a knife that is a poor fit.

Handling fish in the kitchen is a matter of common sense. Keep work surfaces completely clean and do not cross-contaminate foods by preparing vegetables on the same cutting board where you've just trimmed your fish unless you wash it first with hot soapy water. Wash your hands, knives, and other tools frequently and have plenty of clean tea towels available.

Several sauces in this book call for raw eggs or raw egg yolks, ingredients I consider absolutely essential in certain recipes. These days, though, you can't offer such ingredients without a disclaimer, so here's mine (the publisher's is on page ii): Buy good eggs and store them properly. I buy eggs only at farmers' markets and I talk to the farmers about the chickens who lay them to be certain that they are fed a vegetarian diet and have plenty of space for roaming, pecking, and scratching. The few documented instances of contamination have been at huge egg farms where chickens are kept in small cages in rooms that are lit twenty-four hours a day so that the hens will lay more eggs. I do not believe that wholesome food can be produced in such appalling conditions and so I don't buy it; danger of contamination is just one of my considerations. This philosophy guides me in nearly all of my food purchases, and I am entirely comfortable with any risks I may be taking by using ingredients such as raw eggs that humans have relied upon for centuries. In all of my years of cooking I have never once gotten sick, nor made anyone else ill.

Finally, let's consider just what a recipe is, really. A recipe is a story, one traveler's tale of how to get from one point to another. There are other ways to get to the same place. As late as the 1920s and 1930s, recipes were passed on almost as gossip, without a detailed list of ingredients and set-by-step instructions. There was no fast food; most people ate nearly every meal at home. Over the last several decades, recipes have been codified, home cooks have grown increasingly insecure in the kitchen, many people never cook, and today we eat more meals in restaurants than we do at home. I urge you to relax, to enjoy the pleasure of the journey as much as you hope to enjoy the final destination, and to learn to rely upon your own senses and knowledge as much as you rely upon any written recipe. Think of the steps of a recipe as training wheels. Once you get your balance, you don't even notice they've been removed.

A Note on Wines and Other Drinks

The recommendations offered by the restaurants reflect the growing interest in pairing foods with wines so that both are enhanced. In some cases, the wine mentioned may be difficult, or impossible, to find. Many wines are produced in small quantities and are available for only a brief time. Some restaurants have large cellars and are able to hold on to wines for years; they also have access to wines that are never available in retail markets. I have included these recommendations because they are interesting to wine aficionados and because they offer helpful signposts. If you can't find a given wine, ask your wine merchant to suggest something similar. The more general recommendations present a variety of options for wines and other beverages that are easily affordable and readily available.

A BRIEF HISTORY OF SAN FRANCISCO SEAFOOD

"San Francisco is all things to all people, but to the cognoscenti everywhere and anywhere, it is a city of gracious living, which is to say, good eating."

—Herb Caen, in the Foreword to *Golden Gate Gourmet*

I IT ALL BEGINS LONG BEFORE FIRST LIGHT with the fishing boats motoring out through the Golden Gate, their silvery wakes trailing like kites' tails, to return three and four days later with their icy bounty. Regulations require that commercial boats be at least three miles off the coast before they begin fishing. Most go out fifty to one hundred miles, usually traveling in small groups of three or four boats, a floating community that keeps in touch by radio and shares information about where the fish are. The boats are moderately sized, with crews of just two or three.

Some of the boats are trawlers, with huge nets that drag along the bottom or at midlevel, ensnaring petrale sole, English sole, Dover sole, rockfish such as black gill, chile pepper, and thornyhead, and sand dabs.

Fishermen must monitor each species carefully to be certain not to catch more than the monthly limit, which varies from fish to fish. A fisherman may catch as many sand dabs as he wants, for example. "Nowhere else in the country do people enjoy sand dabs as they do in San Francisco," Paul Johnson of Monterey Fish Market explains; the demand is small elsewhere because so little is shipped out of the city. Rockfish, on the contrary, are very limited. The fish is iced when it is caught, and processed—cleaned and cut—on shore. Only salmon fishermen work differently, fishing with a line and cleaning the fish shortly after it is caught. These same fishermen trap Dungeness crabs in the winter months, when salmon is out of season.

After a fisherman has caught his limit, he returns through the Gate, his boat laden with thousands of pounds of fish, and docks at one of the Bay's two operating piers. Fish is sold before it leaves the boat, often to the same distributor year after year. Pier 45, whose cavernous structures were built with federal disaster funds following the Loma Prieta earthquake in 1989, houses nearly a dozen distributors and processors and receives much of the local catch. The distributors buy from the fishermen and deliver the fish to restaurants, markets, and other distributors throughout northern California and beyond. There are a few more distributors at the ramshackle Pier 33, and a large wholesaler on Cesar Chavez Street.

The price is not controlled by the state as is the price of, say, milk; it's governed by demand and competition. "We give [the fishermen] a good price, we promote their fish, and we distribute it. If we do a good job, they stay with us," explains Mike Lucas, who founded North Coast Fisheries at Pier 45 in 1993. Most customers are regulars who trust the quality that comes with dealing with a single distributor. There are buyers who shop around, who examine the catch and buy from various vendors, but they don't necessarily get the best fish because they haven't built up a relationship. If the catch is limited, a loyal customer is going to get the premium fish, not a stranger shopping for a deal.

Like most of the vendors at Pier 45, North Coast Fisheries is primarily a distributor. A secondary enterprise for the firm is processing fish, which consists primarily of filleting it, mostly for the company's own customers but some for other companies. The waste—the heads, tails, gills, and guts—is sold to a tallow company in Crescent City, where it is made into fish oil and fish emulsion used as fertilizer.

II   THE BAY WAS ONCE THE SOURCE of a tremendous quantity of seafood, much of it caught by Chinese fishermen. When work on the Central Pacific Railroad ended in 1869, some Chinese immigrants returned to their homeland, some found work in the goldfields, and others got jobs in vineyards and wineries. Those who had come from the fishing villages of Canton, where they had fished the waters of the Pearl and Yangtze Rivers, returned to fishing, using their skills in the fertile bays and deltas of northern California, and in the process setting up dozens of small villages. No one knows exactly when the first village was founded, but there were several as early as the 1860s. By the beginning of the twentieth century, the San Francisco–San Pablo Bay was ringed by nearly three hundred Chinese fishing villages. Today, only China Camp in northern Marin County remains; it is now a museum and a state park, the only such site in the state devoted to fish and one of only two that focus on the history of Chinese immigrants.

In the mid-nineteenth century, Yugoslav immigrants settled in western Marin County and launched a commercial fishing industry at Tomales Bay, where the local oyster industry now thrives. These immigrants founded the village of White Gulch in the dunes that separate Tomales Bay from the Pacific, and sent their catch of bass, smelt, herring, perch, shrimp, and halibut to San Francisco by train and boat. When the Great Depression came and the price of so much of the catch plummeted, a few resourceful fishermen turned to the infamous white shark, still seen frequently in these waters. While the shark was worth only five cents a pound as fresh fish, its liver, prized by laboratories for its high vitamin content, caused the price of the whole fish to skyrocket to a dollar a pound.

In 1931, Nick Kojic, one of the most successful fishermen in Tomales Bay, loaded his six boats, a two-bedroom house, two wharves, and a pile of fishing nets onto a barge and floated them across the bay from White Gulch to what was to become Nick's Cove. The document that deeded him land stipulated that he could operate neither a grocery store nor an automobile service station, so he opened a seafood restaurant instead, in what had been Jeremiah Blake's old herring smokehouse. For decades, Nick's Cove thrived as a restaurant, bar, informal community center, and dance hall. In 1999, it was sold to Pat Kuleto, the well-known San Francisco restaurateur who also owns the visually dazzling Farallon, one of the city's most popular seafood restaurants.

The San Francisco Bay

At low tide, San Francisco Bay has a shoreline nearly 100 miles long and encompasses about 450 square miles of water. It extends southeast from the Golden Gate for 40 miles, and northeast for 10 miles, to San Pablo Bay. At its greatest width, it is 13 miles wide, with a maximum depth of 36 fathoms, or 216 feet. More than two-thirds of the bay is just 12 feet deep or shallower. It has four major islands: Alcatraz, Angel, Treasure, and Yerba Buena; and seven bridges: Golden Gate, Richmond–San Rafael, San Mateo, Dunbarton, Carquinez, Benicia, and San Francisco–Oakland Bay. There were once toll-booths in both directions, but today, the bridges allow free passage in one direction.

South of San Francisco, at Monterey Bay, the fishing industry was established by Portuguese whalers. In the 1860s, after the Portuguese fishermen had abandoned their whaling stations, Chinese immigrants began fishing here, drying their catch and shipping it to their homeland. When Italian immigrants came to Monterey in the 1880s, they sold their catch fresh in San Francisco, providing the raw ingredients that would inspire so many signature seafood specialties, from shrimp and crab Louis to cioppino. Japanese immigrants arrived in the 1890s and fished primarily for abalone and salmon, and to a lesser degree for the sardines that would soon become so important to the region. The Japanese delivered most of their catch to Monterey's fledgling canneries.

The only seafood fished commercially today in the San Francisco Bay are anchovies, and most go for bait. Across a small channel from Pier 45 is a floating bait receiver where the anchovies are kept, waiting for the fisherman who will buy them at twenty-five dollars a scoop. Anchovies, sardines, and squid for human consumption are processed to the south in Salinas, where both labor and land are cheaper. A lot of employees and a lot of cooler and freezer space are needed to process these fish.

Even though the Bay itself no longer yields much fish, San Francisco is a tremendously important hub for seafood. The local seafood industry stretches from Moss Landing in the south to Fort Bragg in the north, encompassing much more than the famous Bay and immediate coast. Fish from around the world pass through the San Francisco International Airport, arriving from, say, New Zealand or Ecuador within two or three days of being caught. Live scallops come from the East Coast and Canada; live lobster from Maine; yellowtail, grouper, and sea bass from Mexico; and farmed salmon from British Columbia. This international harvest augments the local catch, providing our restaurants with a year-round supply of fine seafood.

III   SAN FRANCISCANS HAVE ALWAYS LOVED OYSTERS. From the gold rush through the early twentieth century, oysters were devoured in great numbers, both raw and in a wealth of dishes, many created by chefs in San Francisco's grand hotels. Among the most celebrated specialties of the time were the oyster omelet, filled with a hundred Olympia oysters, which was served at the Ladies' Grill at the Palace Hotel; oyster loaf; and, of course, Hangtown Fry.

Back then, the Bay teemed with the diminutive Olympia, the only oyster native to the eastern Pacific, and one of the finest tasting oysters in the world. But by the middle of the twentieth century, pollution, overharvesting, and sediment had forced oyster farming to other sites. Today in San Francisco, restaurants serve oysters from Oregon, Washington, and New England, as well as from nearby Tomales Bay, where Hog Island Shellfish Company raises its scrumptious Sweetwaters and Kumamotos.

Olympias are now raised only in Washington State, but the prized oyster may be in trouble. Growers say that they plan to discontinue farming the shellfish. Production costs are too high, they explain, and no one wants to shuck the oysters, which are rarely bigger than a quarter and often smaller. This news should put aficionados on alert: *Eat more Olympias!* Perhaps if demand rises, growers will give up their plan to abandon these succulent little shellfish.

IV   THE DISAPPEARANCE OF FISH and shellfish species remains an ongoing problem for fisheries around the world, though with certain species there have been improvements in recent years. West Coast wild salmon, for example, has come back because the season for it is strictly regulated. Some people feel it may be environmentally harmful to eat wild salmon—aren't they endangered?—but the industry is carefully monitored to ensure its continued viability. Salmon are counted and, if their numbers are low, the opening of the season is delayed. If the population of a particular species—there are five on the West Coast: silver, chum, coho, sockeye, and king—is too low, fishing is forbidden entirely.

Salmon is a renewable resource, its life cycle both short and interesting. After a fish hatches upstream, it travels from river to sea, feeds for two or three years (occasionally four or—rarely—five) and then returns to its birthplace to spawn and die. By the time a wild salmon is caught it is already thinking about the river. If it escapes the fisherman's hook, it eventually finds its river and begins to swim upstream. Once it enters fresh water, remarkable changes take place—essentially, it begins to rot; its flesh softens and its gums shrink, revealing sharp teeth in some species. Its skin changes color and the fish develops a hooked nose that resembles a bird's beak. By the time it spawns, it is already near death, which comes quickly. The dead salmon rots in the creek or stream where it spawns, its carcass providing nourishment for its progeny, as the process begins all over again.

People tend to think salmon is salmon, and don't understand that there are different species that vary in taste and texture and that farmed salmon, which is what is available in most markets most of the time, is inferior to wild. In the mid-twentieth century, even wild California salmon developed a poor reputation because the boats stayed out longer then, holding the fish in icy water. By the fourth day or so, a salmon's flesh was waterlogged and, by the time the consumer got it home, it was mushy. Shorter trips and more careful handling have eliminated the problem. Today California has some of the finest wild king salmon in the world, though it still struggles against its lingering poor reputation. The flavor, texture, and nutritional value of wild salmon are far superior to those of farmed fish and, because regulation of the industry is based on census figures that are closely watched, wild fish are better for the environment too. Numerous problems are associated with farmed fish, including rampant disease and the overuse of antibiotics.

If the California Department of Fish and Game can do a good job with salmon, it can perhaps save other fish, though Mike Lucas feels that much of the regulation has been too little, too late. Lingcod has been harvested nearly to extinction because for years fisherman were allowed to take it when the fish were full of eggs. "You don't take a fish when it has twenty-five pounds of eggs in it," he says, "just like you don't slaughter a pregnant cow." Now commercial fishing for lingcod is a thing of the past, a fate that may await the petrale sole industry. There are two to three months when the petrale sole season should be closed because the fish are spawning, but currently there are no restrictions.

V   WHAT WILL BE THE FATE of the San Francisco seafood industry? Pier 45 surely has strengthened it, and careful management could shepherd struggling fish populations back to health. Fish are also influenced by long cycles, by weather and currents and mysteries taking place far beneath the sea's turbulent surface that we are only now beginning to comprehend. In the meantime, as scientists work to understand the ocean's rhythms and seasons, we can be watchful, encourage wise regulation, and enjoy the distinctive pleasures that only fresh seafood expertly prepared can impart. If you love seafood and even if you never do anything more than grill a fillet of fresh wild salmon at home, you'll relish the glimpse *San Francisco Seafood* gives into the kitchens of some of the city's finest restaurants as chefs find their inspiration in the sea's bountiful harvest, its succulent gifts.

ABSINTHE

Ross Browne
Executive Chef

ABSINTHE IS A LIQUEUR, also known as "the green fairy" and so popular at the turn of the nineteenth century in France that the cocktail hour was called *l'heure verte,* "the green hour," a reference to the alluring green hue of the licorice-flavored elixir. Popular in San Francisco in the bohemian clubs and restaurants of North Beach as late as 1914, absinthe had been banned in nearly every country in the world by about 1910, a result of what seems to have been the French equivalent of Prohibition—France would never have banned all alcohol—and mass hysteria. By the next fin de siècle, the 1990s, it had made a bit of a comeback: Today, the beverage is legal in England, Japan, Portugal, Spain, Andorra, and the Czech Republic, and is occasionally available elsewhere, including San Francisco; and its name is given to restaurants, like this luxurious brasserie in Hayes Valley.

Among the seafood served here is a French-style *fruits de mer* platter piled with oysters, mussels, shrimp, and Dungeness crab, just the sort of dish to encourage the lingering that Absinthe's decor and ambiance invite. For the best experience, ask to be seated in one of the plush, curving velvet banquettes, so cozy you might be inclined to lose yourself until the end of the next century. Absinthe is one of the best places in San Francisco for late-night dining.

398 HAYES STREET
(415) 551-1590

Roasted Sea Bass with Marinated Onions, Polenta, and Olive-Shallot Vinaigrette

True saltwater bass has a delicate flavor that is enhanced by the intensely flavored vinaigrette that dresses it. Do not overcook the bass, or its flesh will become dry.

Polenta Batons

Creamy Polenta (page 213)
1 tablespoon minced fresh sage
1 tablespoon minced fresh thyme
1 tablespoon minced fresh flat-leaf parsley
Freshly ground pepper to taste

2 yellow onions, cut into very thin rounds
Olive oil for roasting plus $1/4$ cup
Kosher salt for sprinkling, plus more to taste
2 tablespoons sherry vinegar
6 tablespoons extra virgin olive oil, plus more for drizzling
1 teaspoon red pepper flakes
1 teaspoon minced garlic (about 2 cloves)
4 whole sea bass, 1 to $1^1/_2$ pounds each, pan-dressed
Freshly ground pepper to taste
1 bunch escarole
Olive-Shallot Vinaigrette Dressing (recipe follows)

Preheat the oven to 450°. Drizzle olive oil on a baking sheet, spread the onions on top, sprinkle with salt, and toss with your fingers to distribute the salt. Roast until the onions are golden brown on top, about 5 minutes. Using a metal spatula, turn the onions over and roast 5 minutes more, or until uniformly browned. Transfer to a medium bowl. In a small bowl, whisk together the vinegar, the 6 tablespoons extra virgin olive oil, the red pepper flakes, and garlic. Pour over the onions and marinate at room temperature for 2 hours.

Make the polenta and, while it is still hot, stir in the herbs and pepper. Brush a 9 by 13-inch rimmed baking sheet with olive oil, pour in the polenta, and smooth with a rubber spatula. Cover with plastic wrap, pressing so that the wrap touches the polenta's surface. Set aside for at least 2 hours, until the polenta is very firm.

Rinse the fish thoroughly inside and out with cool water and drain on tea towels or absorbent paper. Make 3 diagonal cuts across both sides of each fish, cutting not quite to the bone, and drizzle a little extra virgin olive oil into each cut. Season inside and out with salt and pepper.

Preheat the oven to 450° and cut the polenta into 2 by $1/2$-inch batons. Pour a $1/8$-inch-deep layer of olive oil into a rimmed baking sheet, heat it in the oven for 5 minutes, and add the polenta batons in a single layer. Return to the oven and bake until the bottom side of the polenta is golden brown, about 8 minutes. Turn the polenta over, return to the oven, and cook about 8 minutes more, or until both sides are golden brown.

Meanwhile, heat the $1/4$ cup olive oil in a saucepan over medium-low heat. Add the escarole, season with salt and pepper to taste, cover and cook, tossing once or twice, until wilted, about 10 minutes. Remove from the heat. Cover and set aside to keep warm.

Place the fish on a baking sheet and bake for 8 to 10 minutes, or until the flesh flakes away from the bone when poked with a wooden skewer. To serve, place a whole fish on each of 4 plates, placing it off center. Add several polenta batons to each plate and spoon vinaigrette over both the polenta and the bass. Add a mound of escarole, drizzle some juice from the marinated onions over it, garnish the fish with the onions, and serve immediately.

SERVES 4

Olive-Shallot Vinaigrette

$1/4$ cup niçoise olives, rinsed, dried, pitted, and diced
1 shallot, minced
Grated zest of 1 orange
$1/4$ cup champagne vinegar
1 cup extra virgin olive oil
Freshly ground pepper to taste

Combine the olives, shallot, orange zest, and vinegar in a medium bowl. Let stand for 15 minutes. Whisk in the olive oil to make an emulsified sauce. Season with pepper. Taste and correct the seasoning.

MAKES 1 $1/2$ CUPS

Ahi à la Mirabeau with Braised Artichokes

Ross Browne serves this dish in the spring, when California artichokes are at their peak. Alongside, he often offers potato-green garlic gratin. This preparation was inspired by and pays tribute to a classic French dish, filet mignon with anchovy butter.

Anchovy Butter

$1/2$ cup (1 stick) unsalted butter, at room temperature
1 to 2 teaspoons minced anchovies
$3/4$ teaspoon minced shallot
1 tablespoon freshly squeezed lemon juice
Pinch of cayenne pepper
Freshly ground pepper to taste

3 tablespoons butter
2 leeks, including pale green parts, washed and cut into fine julienne
4 cloves garlic, minced
Kosher salt and freshly ground pepper to taste
4 thyme sprigs
1 bay leaf
4 large artichokes, trimmed, quartered, and cored
$1/2$ cup water
Four 6-ounce ahi tuna steaks

To Drink

Dry Rosé
Absinthe recommends: 1998
Domaine de l'Hortus, Languedoc, France

Garnish

4 anchovy fillets, preferably salt-cured, rinsed and drained
$1/2$ cup niçoise olives
4 small sprigs tarragon

To make the anchovy butter, put the butter in a small bowl and use a whisk or wooden spoon to beat it until it turns nearly white. Add the anchovies, shallot, and lemon juice. Season with cayenne and pepper. Set aside.

Melt the 3 tablespoons butter in a deep sauté pan over medium-low heat. Add the leeks and cook, stirring occasionally, until very tender, about 10 minutes. Add the garlic, cook for 2 minutes, and season with salt and pepper. Add the thyme and bay leaf, and arrange the artichokes on top. Add the water, cover, and cook slowly until the hearts of the artichokes are tender when pierced with a fork or a wooden skewer, 20 to 25 minutes.

Meanwhile, prepare a fire in a charcoal grill. Or, just before cooking, heat a stovetop grill pan over medium-high heat. Season the tuna with salt and pepper to taste and grill on one side for 3 to 4 minutes. Turn and grill until just seared, another 2 to 3 minutes. The tuna should be seared on the outside and virtually raw inside.

To serve, divide the braised artichokes among individual warmed serving plates, add a tuna steak to each plate, and top with a generous spoonful of anchovy butter. Garnish with anchovy fillets, olives, and tarragon, and serve immediately.

SERVES 4

Sand Dabs with Sauce Grenobloise

Sand dabs are more popular in San Francisco than anywhere else in the world. In this recipe, the tangy preserved lemons of the sauce provide a perfect contrast to the fish's remarkably sweet flesh. If you have trouble getting sand dabs, use rex sole or any other small flat fish, such as petrale sole.

8 sand dabs, 8 to 10 ounces each, pan-dressed
Kosher salt to taste, plus 3 tablespoons
Freshly ground pepper
$^1/_4$ cup dried currants
$^1/_2$ cup sherry vinegar
$^1/_2$ cup hot water
$1^1/_4$ pounds small new potatoes
Sauce Grenobloise (recipe follows)
$^1/_4$ cup Clarified Butter (see page 201) or olive oil
Flour for dredging
2 bunches spinach, washed and stemmed
$^1/_4$ cup pine nuts, lightly toasted (see page 216)
3 tablespoons minced fresh flat-leaf parsley for garnish

To Drink*

Sauvignon Blanc
Absinthe recommends: 1999
Thornbury Sauvignon Blanc, New
Zealand

Season the sand dabs on both sides with salt and pepper to taste and set aside.

Put the currants in a medium bowl, add the vinegar and water, and let sit for 30 minutes. Put the potatoes in a pot, add water to cover by 2 inches and add the 3 tablespoons of kosher salt. Bring to a boil over high heat, decrease the heat to medium, and simmer until the potatoes are tender, 15 to 25 minutes, depending on their size. Drain thoroughly. Put in a medium bowl, toss with a little of the grenobloise sauce, and keep warm.

Melt half of the clarified butter in a large sauté pan over medium-high heat. Dredge 4 of the sand dabs in flour and fry until golden brown on the bottom, 4 to 5 minutes. Turn and fry until golden brown on the second side, 3 to 4 minutes more. Using a slotted metal spatula, transfer the sand dabs to a platter and keep warm. Cook the remaining sand dabs.

Melt the remaining clarified butter in the same pan over medium heat. Add the spinach and sauté, tossing frequently, until it is wilted, 2 to 3 minutes. Drain the currants, discarding the liquid, and add them to the spinach, along with the pine nuts. Toss, season with salt and pepper to taste, and remove from the heat.

To assemble, place 2 sand dabs on each of 4 warmed dinner plates, then add some of the potatoes and spinach to each portion. Quickly heat the remaining grenobloise sauce in the same sauté pan, spoon it over each portion, garnish with parsley, and serve immediately.

SERVES 4

Sauce Grenobloise

....

8 preserved lemon slices (see page 215), diced, or 1 whole lemon, peeled, seeded, and diced
$^1/_4$ cup capers, rinsed, drained, and dried
$^1/_4$ cup thinly sliced green onion, white part only
$^1/_2$ cup (1 stick) unsalted butter at room temperature

In a bowl, mix together all the ingredients. Set aside until ready to use.

MAKES ABOUT 1 CUP

ANCHOR OYSTER BAR

Todd Nathan Thorpe
Chef

Anchor Oyster Bar is easy to overlook. With its subdued storefront on Castro Street and its casual diner look, you might be inclined to pass it by and head for a flashy eatery, one of the scores of trendy new places where it's as important to see and be seen as it is to eat, and where you will likely be as dazzled by the efforts of the architect as you are by the performance of the chef. But you'll miss out if you do.

Anchor has been offering classic San Francisco seafood, robust and homey and just plain good, for over twenty years. On weekend mornings, you might see bleary-eyed young guys downing oyster shooters in an attempt to alleviate a hangover. You'll see regulars savoring oysters on the half shell— over three dozen varieties are served throughout the year—big bowls of steamer clams, and the oyster loaves for which the city is famous. Anchor's soups and chowders have a subtle literary flourish: The oyster stew, chef Todd Thorpe explains, is virtually identical to one in M. F. K. Fisher's *Consider the Oyster,* and a cod chowder was inspired by *Moby-Dick.* No San Francisco seafood experience is complete without at least one visit to Anchor. Many food lovers, myself among them, count it as one of their favorite locations.

579 Castro Street
(415) 431-3990

San Francisco Oyster Loaf

A sandwich of oysters nestled in a loaf of sourdough bread is an old San Francisco tradition, dating back to restaurants such as Maye's Oyster House, which opened in 1867. A version known as "The Squarer" was made in a hollowed-out loaf smeared with butter, toasted, filled with oysters, wrapped in wax paper and, according to at least one historian, eaten to stave off the effects of a night of overindulgence. Anchor serves its oyster loaf with classic creamy coleslaw, the refreshing crunch of which is an appealing counterpoint to the rich sandwich.

To Drink

India pale ale

Anchor recommends: Tocaloma Pale Ale, Lagunitas Brewing Co., Petaluma

1 sourdough roll

2 cloves garlic, cut in half

2 tablespoons unsalted butter at room temperature

$1/2$ cup fresh bread crumbs, toasted (see page 217)

$1/2$ teaspoon kosher salt

Freshly ground pepper to taste

6 to 8 large oysters, shucked (see page 221)

2 tablespoons heavy whipping cream

Pinch of cayenne pepper

1 teaspoon freshly grated Parmesan cheese

Preheat the oven to 400°. Cut the roll in half lengthwise about $1/4$ inch down from the top. Pull out the soft interior of the bottom half of the roll. Place both halves on a baking sheet and toast the roll, turning once, until lightly browned, about 5 minutes. Rub the inside with the garlic and spread with 1 tablespoon of the butter. Set aside.

In a bowl, mix together the bread crumbs, salt, and pepper. Add the oysters and toss gently until they are thoroughly coated. Melt the remaining 1 tablespoon of butter in a large sauté pan over medium heat until it foams. Add the oysters all at once, being careful not to crowd them (if crowded, they will steam and the coating will become soggy). Fry until browned on the bottom, 2 to 3 minutes; turn and brown on the other side. Carefully transfer the oysters to the hollowed half of the roll. Drizzle the cream over the top and sprinkle with the cayenne and cheese. Place in the sauté pan and bake in the oven for 3 to 4 minutes, or until the cheese is just melted. Top with the other half of the roll and serve immediately, with coleslaw on the side if you like.

SERVES 1

Anchor's Shellfish Salad

You may vary the quantities of the various shellfish in this salad—for example, use all black mussels, omit the calamari, use whatever crab you have available—and still have a wonderful dish. Be sure to read about cooking and cleaning crab on page 220 before you begin.

$3/4$ cup extra virgin olive oil

8 large cloves garlic, minced

4 sprigs thyme

1 teaspoon dried oregano

Generous pinch of red pepper flakes

2 pounds littleneck or Manila clams, scrubbed

1 cup dry white wine

2 pounds black mussels, scrubbed and debearded if necessary (see page 220)

1 pound greenlip mussels, scrubbed and debearded if necessary (see page 220)

8 ounces calamari, cleaned and sliced (see page 219)

1 pound jumbo shrimp, shelled and deveined (see page 219)

1 Dungeness crab, about $1^1/_2$ pounds, cooked, cleaned, and cracked into 8 to 10 pieces (see page 220)

Grated zest of 5 to 6 lemons (about 4 tablespoons)

Juice of 5 to 6 lemons (about $3/4$ cup)

1 cup minced fresh flat-leaf parsley

Kosher salt and freshly ground pepper to taste

10 cups mixed salad greens

2 lemons, cut into wedges, for garnish

To Drink
Stout, porter
Anchor recommends: Pinot Grigio

Heat $1/4$ cup of the olive oil in a large, heavy, nonreactive pot over medium heat. Add half the garlic and sauté until fragrant but not browned. Add the thyme, oregano, pepper flakes, clams, and wine. Cover the pan and steam until the clams just open, 3 to 5 minutes. Using a slotted spoon, transfer the clams to a chilled large bowl. Add the mussels to the liquid, cover, and cook until they just open, 3 to 5 minutes. Transfer them to the bowl with the clams. Discard any clams or mussels that do not open. Add the calamari and shrimp to the pot, cover, and cook until the calamari is just barely opaque and the shrimp are pink, 2 to 3 minutes. Transfer to the bowl of shellfish and reserve the cooking liquid. Add the crab to the bowl. Toss the shellfish with the lemon zest, lemon juice, remaining $1/2$ cup olive oil, remaining garlic, and the parsley. Season with salt and pepper, and toss again very gently. If the mixture seems a little dry, add 2 or 3 tablespoons of the cooking liquid. Cover the salad tightly with plastic wrap and refrigerate to chill thoroughly, at least 1¹/₂ hours.

Place the salad greens on individual plates, divide the shellfish over the greens, and serve immediately with lemon wedges.

SERVES 4 TO 6

A Guide to Bay Area Oysters

Oysters were so popular in the 1800s that the period has been called the "oyster century." Many wild beds were wiped out by overharvesting. Before this time, Native Americans had harvested native oysters for centuries. San Francisco Bay's supply of West Coast Olympia oysters was exhausted during the gold rush years. According to several sources, oysters were planted in the bay almost by accident, when a seafood distributor, M. B. Moraghan, was unable to sell a large shipment of shellfish from the East Coast. To save them for a year, he planted them in a southern portion of San Francisco Bay, where they thrived. By 1895, oysters were the top-grossing seafood in the Bay Area, a boom that lasted only until 1904, when production began to decline. The 1906 San Francisco earthquake is said to have warmed the bay floor to the detriment of the oysters, and sediment caused by nearby development began burying the beds. By the late 1930s, the industry had vanished entirely. Today, oysters are cultivated in Tomales Bay, northwest of San Francisco.

Belon: Although Belon is a protected French designation and California growers are officially prohibited from using it, the highly prized oyster is usually referred to by this name. Officially, the *Ostrea edulis* is known as a European flat or plate oyster in California.

Hog Island Sweetwater: This trademarked name refers to the common *Crassostrea gigas*, the most common cultivated oyster in California waters. It is characterized by its mild, sweet flavor and its deep cup, which facilitates both serving these oysters on the half shell and barbecuing them, because the cup keeps the tasty liquor from draining away.

Kumamoto: This small, plump Japanese oyster, the *Crassostrea sikamea*, is now cultivated in California.

Miyagi: An alternate name for *Crassostrea gigas*; it refers to the Japanese company that provided the original oyster seed to growers on the West Coast.

Olympia: Once common in San Francisco Bay, the tiny *Ostrea lurida* now is harvested only off the coast of Washington State.

Triploid: A newly developed genetic strain of sterile oyster, beneficial because it stays firm, meaty, and lean in the warm summer months, when other oysters soften up and become milky as they prepare to spawn.

Fisherman's Stew with Garlic Sourdough Toast

Anchor Oyster Bar serves portions the average eater might find daunting, dispelling myths of California cuisine's stingy nature and delighting customers at the same time. This hearty stew can easily serve as many as eight hungry diners.

$1/_2$ cup olive oil

2 yellow onions, diced

1 red bell pepper, stemmed, seeded, and diced

5 cloves garlic, minced

Kosher salt and freshly ground pepper to taste

1 tablespoon dried thyme

1 tablespoon dried oregano

1 bay leaf

1 star anise pod

1 cup dry red wine

Two 28-ounce cans crushed tomatoes

One 8-ounce can tomato sauce

1 to 2 tablespoons sugar

2 pounds littleneck or Manila clams, scrubbed

2 pounds black mussels, scrubbed and debearded if necessary (see page 220)

1 pound greenlip mussels, scrubbed and debearded if necessary
    (see page 220)

12 to 18 jumbo shrimp in the shell (see page 219)

2 pounds cod, snapper, or sea bass, or a combination, cut into 2-ounce pieces

Garlic Sourdough Toast (recipe follows)

Heat the olive oil in a large, heavy pot over low heat and cook the onions until very tender, about 10 minutes. Add the bell pepper and cook until tender, 7 to 8 minutes. Stir the vegetables occasionally and do not let them brown. Add the garlic and cook for 2 minutes. Season with salt and pepper, then add the thyme, oregano, bay leaf, and star anise. Add the wine and simmer for 3 to 4 minutes. Stir in the tomatoes and tomato sauce and bring to a boil. Decrease the heat and simmer for 15 minutes. Taste and correct the seasonings. Add enough of the sugar to balance the acid of the tomatoes. The sauce should be quite thick; resist the temptation to thin it. Remove the bay leaf and the anise pod.

If using littleneck clams, add them to the sauce, cover, and simmer for 2 minutes before adding the mussels, shrimp, and fish. If using Manila clams, add all of the shellfish and fish at once, cover the pan, and simmer gently until the clams and mussels are open, 5 to 6 minutes. Discard any clams and mussels that do not open. Ladle into large, warmed soup bowls and serve with garlic sourdough toast.

SERVES 6 TO 8

Garlic Sourdough Toast

$1/_2$ cup (1 stick) salted butter at room temperature
2 cloves garlic, minced
2 tablespoons minced fresh flat-leaf parsley
Pinch of dried oregano
1-pound loaf San Francisco–style sourdough bread, cut in half lengthwise
Pinch of paprika

Preheat the oven to 400°. Melt 1 tablespoon of the butter in a small sauté pan over medium-low heat until foamy. Add the garlic and sauté until fragrant but not browned, about 1 minute. Add the remaining butter, the parsley, and oregano. Remove from the heat and mix together thoroughly. Spread the mixture evenly over the cut surface of the bread and sprinkle paprika on top. Place the bread on a baking sheet and bake until golden brown, about 15 minutes. Cut into thick slices and serve warm.

MAKES 10 TO 12 SLICES

An Illicit Loaf

I shall remember always the mysterious beautiful sensation of well-being I felt, when I was small, to hear my mother talk of the suppers she used to eat at boarding school. They were called "midnight feasts," and were kept secret, supposedly, from the teachers, in the best tradition of the 1890s. They consisted of an oyster loaf.... It was made in a bread loaf from the best baker in the village, and the loaf was hollowed out and filled with rich cooked oysters, and then, according to my mother's vague and yet vivid account, the top of the loaf was fastened on again, and the whole was baked crisp and brown in the oven. Then it was wrapped tightly in a fine white napkin, and hidden under a chambermaid's cape while she ran from the baker's to the seminary and up the back stairs to the appointed bedroom.... The girls, six or seven of them because an oyster loaf was really very large, sat in their best flowered wrappers on the floor, while one of them kept watch on the keyhole and saw that no light flickered from her candle or the shaded lamp.

The maid slipped into the whispering, giggling huddle, and put down her warm bundle, and although she had been well paid was always willing to take a pocketful of the rich cookies the young ladies' mothers sent them every week from home. Then she left, and the oyster loaf was unwrapped.

—M. F. K. Fisher, *Consider the Oyster*

AQUA

Michael Mina
Executive Chef

Rarely do restaurant critics fail to mention the towering floral arrangements at Aqua, nor can they seem to resist talking about the ethereal black mussel soufflé or the audacious yet scrumptious pairing of rare tuna and seared foie gras. Michael Mina, Aqua's inspired executive chef, creates complex, refined, and exuberant seafood dishes in one of the most enchanting dining rooms in all of San Francisco. Indulgence is the rule of the day here, and everything, from the flawless formal service to the visually dazzling presentations, is designed for your pleasure.

If you're looking for an elegant yet enchanting seafood experience, Aqua is your place. Mina's recipes underscore the skill and attention to detail required of a chef producing stylish, complex dishes. Even if you're reluctant to tackle such creations yourself, reading his recipes likely will make you ravenously hungry. Don't be surprised if you find yourself reaching for the phone to call the restaurant for reservations.

252 CALIFORNIA STREET

(415) 956-9662

Savory Black Mussel Soufflé

This soufflé, one of Michael Mina's signature recipes, is a relatively easy one for the novice to tackle because it doesn't collapse quite as thoroughly as more traditional soufflés do. It is absolutely marvelous, with the briny flavors of the mussels mirrored in the reduced cooking liquid used to make the sauce.

To Drink

Sauvignon Blanc
Aqua recommends: 1997 Sylvain
Bailly Sancerre Cuvée Prestige,
Loire Valley, France

2 cups plus 1 bottle (750 ml) chardonnay

8 shallots, minced, plus 5 shallots, minced
 (keep separate)

5 cloves garlic, minced

$1/4$ cup olive oil

1 bunch fresh flat-leaf parsley, stemmed and minced

1 pound black mussels, scrubbed and debearded if necessary
 (see page 220)

$1 1/2$ cups milk

$1/2$ cup (1 stick) unsalted butter, plus 1 tablespoon

$1/2$ cup all-purpose flour

6 egg yolks

10 egg whites

Pinch of kosher salt, plus more to taste

Pinch of cornstarch

$1 1/2$ cups heavy whipping cream

Freshly ground pepper to taste

Pour the 2 cups chardonnay into a small saucepan, add the 8 shallots and the garlic, and simmer over medium heat until almost all of the wine is evaporated. Set aside.

Heat the olive oil in a large sauté pan over medium heat and sauté the 5 shallots until translucent, about 1 minute. Add the parsley and mussels and pour in the bottle of wine. Cover and simmer until the mussels have opened, 5 to 6 minutes. Using a slotted spoon, transfer the mussels to a plate. When they are cool to the touch, remove the mussels from their shells, discarding any that did not open. Mince the mussels and set them aside. Strain the cooking liquid, return it to a clean saucepan, and simmer over medium heat until it is reduced by half, about 15 minutes.

Bring the milk and $1/2$ cup butter to a boil in a medium saucepan over medium heat. Add the flour, stirring constantly until the mixture forms a stiff dough. Continue to cook until it is smooth and shiny, 5 to 7 minutes. Transfer the dough to a mixing bowl and using an electric mixer on low speed, mix for 5 minutes, or until cooled to room temperature. Beat in the egg yolks one at a time; the dough should be bright yellow. Fold in the shallots and the mussels. Set aside.

Preheat the oven to 375°. In a deep bowl, beat the egg whites with the pinches of salt and cornstarch until they form stiff, glossy peaks. Fold into the mussel mixture.

Rub the inside of four 10-ounce soufflé dishes with the 1 tablespoon of butter. Spoon the soufflé mixture into each dish, filling it three-quarters full. Bake for 18 to 21 minutes, or until the tops are golden brown and the soufflés rise $1^1/_2$ inches above the rim of the dish.

Meanwhile, prepare the sauce: Reheat the reduced mussel cooking liquid over medium-high heat. Add the cream and cook to reduce for 5 minutes. Season with salt and pepper.

Place each soufflé dish on a small plate and serve immediately, with the sauce alongside.

SERVES 4

Dungeness Crab Cakes with
Tomato Concassée and Basil Oil

Professional chefs like Michael Mina rely upon a large staff to prepare a complex dish such as these crab cakes. Tackling such a recipe alone in your home kitchen can be daunting, so be sure to allow plenty of time—none of the steps is difficult, but there are several. You can make the mayonnaise and basil oil in the morning (or even the night before), and if you make the cakes in the winter, when Dungeness crab from northern California is at its peak, you might want to omit the tomato concassée. The crab cakes are delicious with or without the basil. You can also substitute a high-quality commercial mayonnaise for the one given here (you'll need $^3/_4$ cup to 1 cup, depending on the thickness of the mayonnaise).

Basil Oil

1 bunch fresh basil, stemmed and washed
$^3/_4$ cup extra virgin olive oil

Mayonnaise

1 egg yolk
1 teaspoon Dijon mustard
2 tablespoons freshly squeezed lemon juice
$^1/_8$ teaspoon cayenne pepper
$^3/_4$ cup extra virgin olive oil
Kosher salt and freshly ground pepper to taste

Tomato Concassée

$^3/_4$ cup extra virgin olive oil
1 clove garlic, minced
10 small shallots, minced
4 cups peeled, seeded, and finely diced tomatoes (about $2^1/_2$ pounds)
    (see page 218)
2 tablespoons balsamic vinegar
$^1/_2$ bunch fresh basil, cut into very thin strips (about 1 cup)
Kosher salt and freshly ground pepper to taste

Crab Cakes

To Drink

Semillon, Viognier
Aqua recommends: 1999 Rockford
Semillon, Barossa Valley, Australia

2 tablespoons olive oil

1 celery stalk, minced

1 small yellow onion, minced

1 pound fresh lump Dungeness crabmeat, picked over
   for shells

2 tablespoons minced fresh flat-leaf parsley

1 tablespoon snipped chives

3 tablespoons panko (Japanese bread crumbs), plus $1^1/_8$ cups

$^1/_4$ cup instant flour (such as Wondra)

4 eggs, beaten

Peanut oil for deep-frying

To make the basil oil, blanch the basil in boiling salted water for 30 seconds. Plunge into salted ice water. Drain and squeeze out the excess water. Put the basil in a blender or food processor and add oil to barely cover. Blend on high speed until a bright green oil is formed. Pour the mixture into a glass or plastic container and let settle for 10 minutes. Strain the oil through several layers of cheesecloth into a clean container, and cover. Use immediately or store in the refrigerator for up to 2 days.

To make the mayonnaise, combine the egg yolk, mustard, lemon juice, and cayenne in a blender or food processor and pulse briefly. With the machine running, add the olive oil in a slow, steady stream. Season with salt and pepper, transfer to a bowl, cover, and refrigerate.

To make the tomato concassée, heat 3 tablespoons of the olive oil in a medium sauté pan over low heat. Add the garlic and shallots and cook until very tender, about 20 minutes. Put the cooked shallots and garlic in a medium bowl, stir in the tomatoes, balsamic vinegar, the remaining olive oil, and the basil, season with salt and pepper, cover the bowl, and set aside for 2 hours. Then strain the tomatoes, put the strained tomatoes in a small bowl, cover, and refrigerate.

To make the crab cakes, heat 1 tablespoon of the olive oil in a small saucepan over low heat and cook the celery and onions until very tender, 15 to 20 minutes. Cool slightly. Combine the onion mixture, crabmeat, mayonnaise, parsley, chives, and the 3 tablespoons panko in a large bowl. Season with salt and pepper and stir to blend. Divide the mixture into 8 equal portions and shape each into a small cake about $^3/_4$ inch thick and 2 inches in diameter.

Put the flour, eggs, and remaining $1^1/_8$ cups panko in separate shallow bowls. Dredge each crab cake first in flour, then eggs, then panko to coat evenly. Set the dredged cakes on a baking sheet, cover, and chill for at least 1 hour and up to 3 hours.

Pour 4 inches of peanut oil into a large heavy skillet and heat to 360°. Cover an oven-proof platter with absorbent paper. In batches of 2 or 3, cook the crab cakes, turning once, until golden brown on both sides, 5 to 6 minutes. Using a slotted metal spoon, transfer the cakes to the lined platter to drain. Keep warm in a low oven while cooking the remaining cakes.

To serve, spoon tomato concassée in the center of each of 4 plates and set 2 crab cakes on top. Drizzle with basil oil and serve immediately.

SERVES 4

The Red Menace

In warm months a phenomenon known as a red tide—which is not a tide, is not red, and has nothing to do with communism—occurs when a one-celled plankton known as a dynoflagellate suddenly blooms—that is, increases rapidly in population. A unique alchemy of sunlight, carbon dioxide, water temperature, and nutrients causes the bloom, a time when filter feeders—any sea creature that extracts nutrients by filtering sea water—can become laden with a toxin found in the plankton. So mussels, clams, and wild oysters (very few of which are harvested anyway) are quarantined during red tides. Careful monitoring of coastal waters is absolutely crucial because the toxin cannot be seen, it cannot be detected by taste or smell, it is not destroyed by cooking or freezing, and when eaten, it causes paralytic shellfish poisoning, a condition that is almost always fatal. There is virtually no risk of buying shellfish contaminated with the toxin or of being served them in restaurants; virtually all deaths occur when amateur harvesters ignore quarantines.

Crispy Sand Dabs with Grits
and Artichoke and Garlic Chips

Because they are so small, sand dabs usually are cooked and served on the bone. Boned sand dabs can be more difficult to prepare well, since fish cooked on the bone retains its moisture. Here, chef Michael Mina employs an interesting technique to offer his guests the luxury of boned sand dabs that are as moist and succulent as bone-in fish. He uses a tangy aioli to hold two fillets together, then breads and fries them. The fish is crispy on the outside but moist all the way through. Because sand dabs are small, it takes a few attempts to get the hang of removing the fillets. If you feel daunted by the task, as your fishmonger to demonstrate it for you. There will be a lot of meat left on the bones, so save them for making fish fumet (page 207). Mina uses just the larger of the two fillets on each fish, so it takes eight fish for four servings. It is more economical, of course, to use both fillets, and it works nearly as well. If you can't find elephant garlic, which is very mild, just use the artichokes.

Red Pepper Syrup

5 red bell peppers, roasted and peeled (see page 219)
$1/2$ cup sugar
$1/2$ cup rice wine vinegar

Artichoke and Garlic Chips

Half a lemon
1 raw artichoke heart, trimmed (see page 202)
1 clove elephant garlic
Peanut oil for deep-frying

Grits

3 cups Chicken Stock (page 205)
1 cup yellow grits
$1^1/_2$ tablespoons mascarpone
$1^1/_2$ tablespoons Roasted Garlic Purée (see page 212)
Kosher salt and freshly ground pepper to taste

Brown Butter Sauce

4 tablespoons unsalted butter

1$\frac{1}{2}$ tablespoons freshly squeezed lemon juice

2 tablespoons Chicken Stock (page 205)

3 tablespoons diced cooked artichoke hearts

2 teaspoons each minced roasted red and yellow bell peppers (see page 219)

1 teaspoon capers

2 tablespoons toasted pine nuts (see page 216)

1 teaspoon kosher salt

1 teaspoon minced fresh flat-leaf parsley

Freshly ground pepper to taste

Sand Dabs

4 sand dabs, 8 to 10 ounces each, pan-dressed

2 tablespoons Aioli (page 211)

2 eggs, beaten

2 cups panko (Japanese bread crumbs)

1 cup Clarified Butter (page 201)

Kosher salt and freshly ground pepper to taste

To make the red pepper syrup, combine all the ingredients in a blender and blend until smooth. Strain through a fine-meshed sieve into a small saucepan. Simmer over medium-low heat until the mixture is reduced to a thick syrup, 20 to 25 minutes. Set aside.

Meanwhile, make the chips. Fill a small bowl with water, squeeze the lemon into it, and set aside. Using a mandoline, slice the artichoke heart very thinly and drop the slices into the acidulated water. Set aside. Half-fill a small saucepan with cold water, slice the garlic very thinly, and drop it into the saucepan. Slowly bring the water to a boil over medium heat. Drain and repeat the process of bringing the garlic to a boil 3 more times. Drain the garlic slices and the artichoke slices thoroughly and use a tea towel to pat them dry.

Half-fill a small heavy saucepan with peanut oil. Heat to 350° over medium heat and carefully fry the artichoke and garlic slices in batches until they are pale golden brown and crispy. Using a slotted spoon, transfer to absorbent paper to drain.

Next, prepare the grits. Bring the chicken stock to a boil in a saucepan over medium heat. Add the grits, stirring constantly to avoid lumps. When the grits begin to thicken, decrease the heat to very low, season with salt and pepper, and cook until the grits are tender, about 30 minutes.

As the grits cook, begin to prepare the sauce by melting the butter in a small sauté pan over medium-low heat until it turns golden brown and has a nutty aroma. Carefully stir in the lemon juice and chicken stock and remove from the heat.

Meanwhile, fillet the sand dabs. Using a very sharp boning knife, cut close to the bone, lifting off the fillets and leaving the skin intact. Each sand dab will yield one larger and one smaller fillet. Set the 4 larger fillets skin side down on a work surface. Spread aioli over the surface of each fillet, and top each fillet with one of the smaller fillets, placing it skin side up and pressing gently so the fillets stick together. Place the beaten eggs and the panko in separate shallow bowls. Dip each doubled fillet into the beaten eggs and then dredge it thoroughly in the panko.

To cook the sand dabs, heat half of the clarified butter in a large sauté pan over medium-high heat. Add 2 of the doubled fillets and fry them until they are golden brown on one side, about 3 minutes. Turn and fry until evenly browned, 2 to 3 minutes more. Using a slotted metal spatula, transfer to a serving platter lined with absorbent paper to drain. Keep hot in a low oven while you cook the remaining 2 doubled fillets. Add more butter to the sauté pan as necessary.

To finish the sauce, return the sauté pan with the browned butter to medium-low heat and when it is hot, stir in the artichoke, peppers, capers, and pine nuts. Season with salt and pepper and remove from heat.

To finish the grits, correct the seasoning and stir in the mascarpone and roasted garlic purée.

Spread the cooked grits in a circle in the center of 4 warmed plates and set a doubled fillet on top. Stir the parsley into the sauce and spoon the sauce on top of the fish and around the grits. Drizzle a little of the red pepper syrup around the plate, scatter the artichoke and garlic chips on top, and serve immediately.

SERVES 4

A. SABELLA'S RESTAURANT

Todd Hansen
Executive Chef

I confess to having a soft spot for A. Sabella's. The first restaurant meal I remember was at this local institution, when I was perhaps five years old. I can still recall every detail, including the slant of buttery light pouring in through a west-facing window. I remember, too, my mother's admonition that no wine be added to my sautéed crab legs. "She's a child," she scolded, as if I were invisible, as if the waiter were incapable of realizing for himself that I was indeed a little kid. Of course, any alcohol would have evaporated in the sauté pan. A suitable compromise was reached, and before long a silver dish bearing eight perfect sections of Dungeness leg meat on a golden lake of butter arrived, surrounded by a cloud of garlicky aromas. I was enchanted, though not for the first time. I'd been eating Dungeness crab—in cocktails, crab Louis, and cioppino, and just plain neat with lemon—since I could remember. Trendier places come and go, but A. Sabella's endures, offering its traditional San Francisco seafood to both tourists and locals.

2766 TAYLOR STREET, THIRD FLOOR

(415) 771-6775

Petrale Sole with Spinach, Brown Butter, and Capers

This popular flatfish, a member of the flounder family, may be in trouble because of year-round harvesting. Even though it is available, I would avoid it during the winter months when the fish is spawning. Chef Todd Hansen recommends frying the fish in garlic-flavored olive oil, but if you don't have any, don't worry. Just mix two tablespoons of olive oil with one clove of garlic that has been put through a press. Let the garlic steep in the oil for about an hour, then strain the oil before using it so that the little bits of garlic don't burn. Your homemade mixture will taste far better than most commercial garlic-flavored oils.

Four 6- to 8-ounce petrale sole fillets
Kosher salt and freshly ground black pepper to taste
Flour for dredging
Garlic-flavored olive oil for sautéing
1 tablespoon olive oil
4 cups spinach leaves, washed
$1/_2$ cup (1 stick) butter, browned (see page 201)
4 ounces bay shrimp
2 tablespoons capers, fried (see note, next page)
3 lemons, peeled and cut into individual segments (see page 218)
$1/_4$ cup coarse bread crumbs, lightly toasted, for garnish (see page 217)
2 tablespoons minced fresh flat-leaf parsley for garnish

To Drink

Sauvignon Blanc, Soave Classico
A. Sabella's recommends: Gainey
Sauvignon Blanc Limited Select,
Santa Ynez Valley

Season the sole on both sides with salt and pepper, and dredge it in flour. Add just enough garlic-flavored olive oil to a large nonstick sauté pan to coat the bottom, heat over medium heat, and sauté the fillets until golden brown, 3 to 4 minutes per side. Transfer to individual plates and keep warm in a low oven.

Add the 1 tablespoon olive oil to the same pan and heat over medium heat. Add the spinach, season with salt and pepper to taste, toss, and cook until wilted, 2 to 3 minutes. Arrange the spinach around each fillet.

Working quickly, heat the browned butter in the same pan over medium heat. Add the shrimp, capers, and lemon segments, heat through, and spoon over fish. Garnish each portion with some of the bread crumbs and parsley and serve immediately.

SERVES 4

Note: To fry capers, heat $1/4$ cup olive oil in a small sauté pan over medium heat. When it is hot, carefully add the capers. Cook the capers, gently agitating the pan, until they plump up and open, about 2 minutes. Use a slotted spoon to transfer the capers to absorbent paper.

The Seafood Restaurants of Fisherman's Wharf

Fisherman's Wharf is one of the premier tourist destinations in all of San Francisco, but its history extends back to long before visitors flocked to the city. Meiggs' Wharf was built in 1853 to provide moorings for the lumber schooners owned by Henry Meiggs, who also owned a sawmill at Mason and Powell Streets. The area's fishermen, who originally sold their catch from a pier at the end of Union Street, under the shadow of Telegraph Hill, moved their operations here in 1900. The first well-known restaurant in Fisherman's Wharf was opened by Giuseppa Bazzuro, from Genoa, Italy, in an abandoned ship, but for a long time, only fishermen ate in the area. Eventually, others came. Tommaso Castagnola, a fisherman, offered the first seafood cocktails for sale, and soon another enterprising fisherman began cooking big pots of clam chowder. Soon, all manner of seafood stalls were attracting customers from all over San Francisco. Today, locals tend to leave this area to the tourists, though it remains a colorful, lively destination, with spectacular views and great places for a walk, even if the food is no longer the most exciting.

A. Sabella's (see page 32).

Alioto's and the **Oysteria**, often claimed to be the birthplace of cioppino. Outside, cracked crab and seafood cocktails.

Café Pescatore, Italian seafood.

Dante's Fresh Italian Seafood, offering swordfish, salmon, halibut, prawns, and, of course, cioppino.

Fisherman's Grotto, with a cracked-crab sidewalk stand outside and retro fare inside, including crab Louis with iceberg lettuce, bubbling crab gratin, and steamed mussels.

Neptune's Palace, with a view of Alcatraz Island and frolicking sea lions and seals.

Pompeii's Grotto, offering Italian seafood since 1946 in an intimate, romantic setting.

Scoma's, popular among tourists and locals alike.

Tarantino's, featuring scallops, sand dabs, rex sole, and abalone.

Tokyo Sukiyaki Restaurant and Sushi Bar, for when cooking fish at all seems going too far.

Roasted Garlic Crab with Grilled Fennel

You'll notice that these instructions for cooking crab vary from those on page 220. Although many techniques and basic recipes are codified, chefs refine classic methods all of the time. These personal flourishes explain why the same recipe prepared by two chefs may be entirely different. Here, the crab is initially undercooked so that it will remain moist during roasting. Be sure to use all the garlic called for.

To Drink

Chardonnay, Orvieto Classico
A. Sabella's recommends: 1997
Chalk Hill Estate Chardonnay,
Sonoma County; 1998 Olivet Lane
Chardonnay, Russian River Valley

1 lemon, cut into quarters
$1/_2$ cup kosher salt
4 live Dungeness crabs, about $1 1/_2$ pounds each
2 fennel bulbs, trimmed, fronds reserved
Olive oil for coating
6 to 8 new potatoes, cooked until tender and sliced
1 cup (2 sticks) unsalted butter
8 ounces garlic (2 to 3 bulbs), cloves separated, peeled, and minced
$3/_4$ cup Pernod
1 lemon, cut into wedges for garnish

Bring a very large pot of water to a boil, add the quartered lemon and kosher salt, and cook the crabs, one at a time, for 4 minutes each. Drain the crabs, let cool to room temperature, and clean and crack them. Break the bodies in half.

Prepare a fire in a charcoal grill or heat a stovetop grill pan. Cut the fennel into $1/_4$-inch-thick lengthwise slices, coat with olive oil, and grill until tender and golden brown, 4 to 5 minutes per side. Transfer the fennel slices to a roasting pan and toss with the sliced potatoes and crab pieces. Mince 2 tablespoons of the fennel fronds and set aside for garnish; discard the rest.

Preheat the oven to 425°. Melt the butter in a small saucepan, add the garlic, stir, and simmer for 4 to 5 minutes. Pour the mixture over the crab, potatoes, and fennel, and roast in the oven until the edges of the crab just begin to turn golden brown, 5 to 6 minutes. Arrange the crab, fennel, and potatoes on a serving platter. Set the roasting pan with its juices aside. Pour the Pernod into a small saucepan. Heat over very low heat, swirling the pan to pick up flavor. Pour the Pernod into the roasting pan and stir to mix in the pan juices and garlic. Pour the liquid over the crab and vegetables, garnish with the minced fennel fronds and lemon wedges, and serve immediately.

SERVES 4

Cioppino

San Francisco is home to a large number of Ligurian immigrants, many of them from Genoa, a famous fishing community on the Italian Riviera. They came, as so many others did, in the mid-1800s with the hope of sharing in the bounty of the gold rush, and stayed as entrepreneurs, restaurateurs, businessmen, and fishermen. The cuisine they brought with them had a tremendous influence on the evolution of both agriculture and cooking in California, especially in and around the Bay Area. Over the decades, many chefs and restaurateurs have laid claim to cioppino as their own or their ancestors' creation, but its roots clearly are in the fishing communities of Northern Italy, where tomato and seafood stew is known as *ciuppin*. Tales of stew simmering aboard small fishing boats as they headed back through the Golden Gate are among the most common lore of early San Francisco, and it's easy to imagine that the dish could never be better than when it is made under such conditions. Back on shore, cioppino was among the first signature dishes served at the city's earliest restaurants at Fisherman's Wharf.

To Drink

Rosé di Bolgheri, Pinot Nero

Broth

3 tablespoons olive oil

1 onion, diced

5 cloves garlic

Kosher salt to taste

1 red bell pepper, seeded, deribbed, and diced

1 green bell pepper, seeded, deribbed, and diced

1 yellow bell pepper, seeded, deribbed, and diced

1 jalapeno chile, seeded and minced

1 sprig oregano

2 sprigs basil

2 sprigs flat-leaf parsley

1 cup dry white wine

2 cups Chicken Stock (page 205)

3 cups Fish Fumet (page 207)

Pinch of saffron threads

2 cups tomato sauce or Tomato Concassée (page 202)

2 cups Fish Fumet (page 207)

2 cooked, cleaned, and cracked Dungeness crabs, each cut into
    8 pieces (see page 220)

8 jumbo shrimp, peeled and deveined (see page 219)

16 Manila clams, scrubbed

16 small black mussels, scrubbed and debearded if necessary
    (see page 220)

1 tablespoon minced fresh flat-leaf parsley for garnish

2 teaspoons minced fresh oregano for garnish

Toasted Garlic Bread (page 214)

To make the broth, heat the olive oil in a large kettle over medium-low heat. Add the onion and garlic, season with salt, and cook for about 10 minutes, stirring occasionally. Add the bell peppers and cook until limp, 4 to 5 minutes. Add the jalapeno, oregano, basil, and parsley, and cook 2 minutes more. Add the wine, bring to a boil, and cook until liquid has nearly completely evaporated, 7 to 8 minutes. Add the chicken stock and simmer until reduced by half, 7 to 8 minutes, and stir in the fish fumet and saffron threads. Simmer for 10 minutes. Strain, discarding the vegetables, and cool. Use right away or cover and refrigerate for up to 2 days.

To make the cioppino, combine the tomato sauce, broth, and fish fumet in a large pot and bring to a low simmer over medium heat. Cover and simmer 10 minutes. Add all of the shellfish and cook, covered, until the mussels and clams open, 3 to 5 minutes. Discard any mussels or clams that do not open. Ladle into large soup bowls, dividing the shellfish evenly among the servings, and sprinkle with parsley and oregano. Serve immediately, with garlic bread alongside.

SERVES 4

BELON

Paul Arenstam
Chef

Belon, with its yellow storefront and inviting display of shell-fish, including the restaurant's namesake oysters, is one of San Francisco's most Parisian eateries. Tucked away on the edge of the Tenderloin, one of the city's seediest neighborhoods, Belon is the sort of place you might discover when there's an unexpected downpour and you duck into the nearest open door. "What a discovery!" you say to yourself.

The cozy atmosphere of the dining room is enhanced by partitions of blond wood that create smaller rooms, spaces that encourage intimate conversation and allow you to savor your meal at a leisurely pace. The cuisine is honest, soulful, and expertly prepared. Belon's young chef and co-owner, Paul Arenstam, worked at Rubicon for five years, and at several of southern California's best restaurants before that. The restaurant is a personal endeavor for which he enlisted a single partner, John Gaul. Many of the city's newer eateries have a decidedly corporate ambiance, with million-dollar interiors, encyclopedic wine lists, and menus that somehow lack the warmth and heart you find when a single person who loves his craft has risked everything to make a go of it. Belon's menu has that personal touch. It's not exclusively seafood; there are voluptuous soups, slow-braised meats, and classic brasserie dishes like chateaubriand garnished with irresistible morsels of bone marrow. The brief wine list offers appealing selections that complement Paul's food perfectly.

25 Mason Street

(415) 776-9970

Mussels à la Meunière and Pommes Frites

At Belon, chef Paul Arenstam serves mussels and frites in the same bowl. The potatoes soak up the tasty mussel juices, which are enriched by the garlicky aioli topping the mussels. Although the restaurant offers this dish as an appetizer, many diners enjoy it as a main course. If you don't feel like messing with the frites, you can make just the mussels—they're quick, easy, and delicious. If you do make the frites, start them one day ahead—the potatoes need to soak overnight—and you'll be very pleased with the results you get from Paul's recipe.

1 pound Kennebec or mature russet potatoes

Peanut oil for deep-frying

3 tablespoons unsalted butter

2 shallots, thinly sliced

6 sprigs thyme

3 pounds small black mussels, scrubbed and debearded
    if necessary (see page 220)

1 cup dry white wine

$^1/_2$ cup Aioli (page 211)

To Drink

Dry Rosé, Sauvignon Blanc
Belon recommends: 1999
H. Reverdy Sancerre; Louie
Metaireau Muscadet Cuvée One

A day before preparing the dish, peel the potatoes and cut them into $^3/_8$ by 4-inch pieces. Put them in a bowl, cover with water, and refrigerate overnight. Drain and dry thoroughly with paper towels. Fill a large, heavy pot or deep fryer half full with peanut oil and heat over medium-high heat to 330°. Carefully plunge a generous handful of potatoes into the oil and stir quickly with a heavy spoon so that the potatoes do not stick together. Cook for 4 minutes and, using a slotted spoon or a wire-mesh skimmer, promptly transfer the potatoes to absorbent paper to drain. Repeat the process to cook the remaining potatoes. Set aside while cooking the mussels. The potatoes can be prepared up to this point 1 to 2 days in advance; cover the potatoes and refrigerate until ready to use. (The partially cooked potatoes can also be frozen, carefully wrapped, for up to 1 month. Thaw frozen potatoes before continuing with the recipe.)

To prepare the mussels: In a large saucepan, melt the butter over medium-high heat, add the shallots and thyme, and sauté for 2 minutes. Add the mussels and cook, agitating the pan, for 1 minute. Increase heat to high, add the white wine, cover, and cook until the mussels open, 3 to 4 minutes. Uncover and simmer until the sauce is slightly thickened, 1 to 2 minutes. Discard the herb sprigs and any mussels that do not open.

Meanwhile, fill a large, heavy pot or deep fryer half full with peanut oil and heat over medium-high heat to 340°. Cook the potatoes in batches until they are golden brown, about 5 to 7 minutes. Using a slotted spoon or a wire-mesh skimmer, transfer to absorbent paper to drain. Season with salt.

To serve, divide the mussels among large serving bowls, placing them in a stack on one side of each bowl. Place some potatoes in a pile next to the mussels. Spoon the mussel sauce over the mussels, top the frites with a generous spoonful of aioli, and serve immediately.

SERVES 4

Petrale Sole with Celery Confit and Sauce Verjus

Petrale sole has long been a staple at seafood restaurants throughout San Francisco. Here, Paul pairs it with an earthy confit of celery, celery root, and potatoes. In an unusual and highly successful flourish, he adds humble Thompson seedless grapes to the simple sauce of tangy verjus and olive oil infused with celery. You can prepare the confit the day before serving the dish; just remove the vegetables from the refrigerator 30 minutes before completing your cooking.

8 to 10 stalks celery, preferably inner stalks, strings removed,
   cut into $1/8$ by 1-inch lengthwise pieces (about 3 cups)

3 sprigs thyme

1 sprig rosemary

1 bay leaf

2 cloves garlic, bruised

1 cup olive oil, plus more as needed to cover celery

3 russet potatoes, peeled and cut into $1/8$ by 1-inch pieces

1 celery root, peeled and cut into $1/8$ by 1-inch pieces

$1/3$ cup verjus (see note, next page)

Four 6-ounce petrale sole fillets, skin removed

Kosher salt and freshly ground pepper to taste

$1/4$ cup all-purpose flour

3 tablespoons Clarified Butter (page 201)

2 tablespoons unsalted butter

1 cup Chicken Stock (page 205)

$3/4$ cup Thompson seedless grapes, cut into very thin rounds

12 to 16 celery leaves from inner stalks for garnish

12 to 16 flat-leaf parsley leaves for garnish

To Drink

Chardonnay

Belon recommends: 1998 Olivier Savary Chablis, Burgundy; 1999 Toad Hollow Chardonnay, North Coast, Francine Selection

Put the celery, thyme, rosemary, bay leaf, and garlic in a small saucepan over very low heat and pour the 1 cup olive oil over it. If the oil does not cover the celery completely, add more to cover. Cook very slowly until the celery is completely tender but not mushy, 8 to 12 minutes. Discard the herb sprigs, bay leaf, and garlic. Using a slotted spoon, transfer the celery to a bowl and set aside. Reserve the oil.

In a large saucepan of salted boiling water, cook the potatoes until just tender, 5 to 7 minutes. Drain thoroughly and add to the bowl with the celery. Cook the celery root in salted boiling water until just tender, 7 to 9 minutes. Drain thoroughly and add to the bowl with the celery and potatoes. Toss the vegetables together gently, put them in a medium saucepan, and set aside. Pour the verjus in a small saucepan and set aside.

Season the fish fillets on both sides with salt and pepper and dust with flour. Heat the clarified butter in a large sauté pan over medium-high heat and cook the fillets for $1\frac{1}{2}$ minutes. Add 1 tablespoon of the unsalted butter and, when it is melted, spoon it over the fillets and cook for 1 minute. Turn the fillets and cook until they are golden brown, about 2 minutes. Transfer to a warm plate and keep warm in a low oven.

Working quickly, pour the chicken stock over the vegetables, place the pan over medium heat, add the remaining 1 tablespoon unsalted butter, and season with salt and pepper to taste. Heat through, agitating the pan occasionally.

Meanwhile, heat the verjus over medium heat and add $\frac{2}{3}$ cup of the reserved olive oil. Carefully taste the mixture and add more of the olive oil if it is too tart, and more verjus if it seems flat. Season with salt and pepper to taste, add the grapes, and immediately remove from the heat.

Divide the celery confit among 4 warmed shallow bowls and top each serving with a fillet. Spoon some sauce over each fillet, garnish with celery and parsley leaves, and serve immediately.

SERVES 4

Note: Verjus, the juice of unripened grapes, has been used in France for centuries. The Fusion brand is made in Napa County and is available in gourmet shops and specialty foods stores.

Skate Wing with Braised Cabbage and Bacon

Skate is an inexpensive fish that has been overlooked by Americans until recently. If you can't find it, ask your butcher or fishmonger to order it for you. You can make the braised cabbage a day or two in advance; let it cool thoroughly after cooking and store it, covered, in the refrigerator. Reheat it over low heat before preparing the skate.

1 large or 2 small heads savoy cabbage, trimmed
    and cut into large dice
8 tablespoons Clarified Butter (page 201)
10 ounces bacon, preferably apple-wood smoked, diced
1 onion, diced
1 cup dry white wine
1 cup Chicken Stock (page 205)
Kosher salt and freshly ground pepper to taste
Four 6-ounce skate wing fillets, cleaned (see page 219)
$1/4$ cup all-purpose flour
6 tablespoons unsalted butter, cut into small cubes,
    plus more if needed
$1/2$ cup sherry vinegar in a squeeze bottle
$1/4$ cup minced fresh flat-leaf parsley

To Drink

Beaujolais, Pinot Noir, Montepulciano d'Abruzzo
Belon recommends: 1998 Patrick et Nathalie Brunet Fleurie, Beaujolais

In a large pot of salted boiling water, cook the cabbage until just tender, 4 to 5 minutes. Drain thoroughly.

In a large saucepan, melt 4 tablespoons of the clarified butter over medium heat, add the bacon, and cook until it is crisp, 8 to 10 minutes. Add the onion, decrease the heat to low, and cook until the onion is very tender, about 15 minutes. Increase the heat to medium-high, add the wine, and cook, stirring occasionally, until the wine is almost completely evaporated, about 5 minutes. Add the cabbage, decrease the heat to low, and stir to thoroughly combine the cabbage with the onion mixture. Add the chicken stock, cover, and cook until the cabbage is very tender, about 20 minutes. Season with salt and pepper. Remove from the heat, set aside, and keep warm.

Place the skate fillets on a work surface and season on both sides with salt and pepper to taste. Dust the fillets lightly with flour. In a large sauté pan, melt the remaining 4 tablespoons clarified butter over medium-high heat. When the butter is very hot, add 2 of the fillets and cook for 45 seconds. Add 2 or 3 small cubes unsalted butter to the pan and, when it is melted, spoon it over the skate and cook for 1 minute more. Turn the fillets over and cook until golden brown, about 2 minutes. Transfer to a plate and keep warm in a low oven while you cook the remaining 2 fillets.

Quickly make the sauce: Heat a small sauté pan over high heat and, when it is very hot, add the remaining butter and cook until it begins to turn brown, 2 minutes or less. Using the squeeze bottle, add most of the vinegar to the butter, squirting it in a circular stream and agitating the pan all the while. Carefully taste the sauce and adjust its acidity; if it is too tart, swirl in a little more butter; if it seems too oily, add a little more vinegar and stir quickly to emulsify the sauce. Stir in the parsley and season with salt and pepper to taste.

To serve, divide the cabbage among 4 warmed large shallow bowls and place a skate fillet on top of each serving. Spoon some sauce over each fillet and serve immediately.

SERVES 4

BIX

Gerard Darian
Executive Chef

EVERYTHING ABOUT BIX IS COOL and posh, from its location on Gold Street, a narrow European-style alley to the cruise-ship décor, stylish mezzanine, and sultry subdued lighting. An enormous painting, *Absinthe: The Butler's in Love,* hangs over the baby grand piano. A torch singer completes the time warp, transporting customers to the era of supper clubs, clandestine liaisons, cocktails, and jazz. The menu is not exclusively seafood, and the restaurant's signature dish is a transcendent chicken hash, but there is more than enough fish, shellfish, and caviar to sustain the illusion that you are dining on a seafaring vessel. In the early evening, Bix is jammed with customers flirting over their famous martinis, considered among the best in the city.

56 GOLD STREET

(415) 433-6300

Grilled Santa Barbara Prawns with Bucatini Timbales and Pea Shoot Purée

Live Santa Barbara spot prawns are a delicacy available for a few weeks in early spring. In March and sometimes April, you find them in tanks in the seafood markets of Chinatown. They are so much better than the frozen prawns offered in most supermarkets that it is worth almost any effort to get them. When you make the timbales, you'll have the best results if you use a premium imported pasta, such as that made by Rustichella d'Abruzzo. In place of ramekins, you can make the timbales in eight-ounce Pyrex bowls; they are the perfect shape and the timbales unmold beautifully.

Bucatini Timbales

8 ounces bucatini pasta

2 ounces sliced pancetta, cut into $1/2$-inch-wide strips

2 tablespoons unsalted butter

2 tablespoons flour

2 cups whole milk

Kosher salt to taste

1 cup toasted bread crumbs (see page 217) or panko
 (Japanese bread crumbs)

1 cup English peas, blanched for 1 minute

3 cups pea shoots

Water as needed

8 Santa Barbara spot prawns in the shell

Olive oil for brushing

Kosher salt and freshly ground pepper to taste

2 tablespoons extra virgin olive oil

2 tablespoons unsalted butter

To make the timbales, cook the bucatini in a large pot of salted boiling water until al dente, about 10 minutes. Drain the pasta thoroughly and put it in a medium bowl. Meanwhile, fry the pancetta in a small sauté pan over medium heat until it is just crisp; do not let burn. Using a slotted spoon, transfer to absorbent paper to drain.

Preheat the oven to 350°. Melt the butter in a medium saucepan over medium heat and add the flour. Stir and cook for 2 minutes. Gradually whisk in the milk, reduce the heat to medium-low, and simmer, stirring constantly with a whisk or wooden spoon, until the sauce thickens, 2 to 3 minutes. Season with salt and remove from the heat.

Smear the inside of four 6-ounce ramekins or ovenproof glass bowls with a generous amount of butter, add some of the bread crumbs, and rotate the ramekins so that they are evenly coated with the crumbs. Shake out the excess and refrigerate until ready to use.

Toss the hot pasta with the pancetta and the peas, pour the sauce over it, and divide it evenly among the ramekins. Using your fingers or a fork, turn the pasta in each ramekin until it forms a circular pattern. Place the ramekins on a baking sheet and bake for 20 minutes, or until the tops of the timbales are just turning golden brown.

Meanwhile, blanch the pea sprouts in a large pot of salted boiling water for 10 seconds. Drain and plunge into ice water for 60 seconds. Drain again. Shake off the excess water, place the sprouts in a blender and blend until smooth, adding cold water as needed to form a loose purée. Pour the purée into a clean medium saucepan.

Heat a grill pan or sauté pan over medium-high heat. Leaving the prawns in their shells, butterfly them, cutting them lengthwise almost but not quite all the way through. Remove the veins. Carefully open up the prawns, brush them very lightly with olive oil, and grill or sauté them until they just turn opaque and pink, about 2 minutes per side. Season with salt and pepper and remove from the heat immediately.

Working very quickly, stir the olive oil into the purée, season it with salt and pepper to taste, and heat it over medium-low heat. Whisk in the butter until incorporated. Remove from the heat.

Unmold each of the timbales onto an individual plate and spoon some of the purée around each one. Lean 2 prawns, tails pointing upwards, against each timbale. Serve immediately.

SERVES 4

Wild King Salmon with Summer Vegetable Ragout

Wild salmon has a sweeter taste and a firmer texture than farmed salmon, so be sure to ask your fishmonger about it before making your purchase. In years when there are plenty of salmon off the California coast, the commercial season runs from around the middle of May until the end of September.

Four 6-ounce fillets wild king salmon, pin bones removed (see page 100)
Kosher salt and freshly ground pepper to taste
About 16 fresh basil leaves, cut into fine shreds
Olive oil for drizzling, plus 1 tablespoon

Ragout and Sauce

2 tablespoons butter
4 to 6 ounces small Blue Lake green beans, blanched for 3 minutes and cut in half lengthwise
8 baby yellow zucchini, quartered lengthwise, blanched for 2 minutes
8 baby green zucchini, quartered lengthwise, blanched for 2 minutes
8 asparagus tips, blanched for 2 minutes
4 to 8 baby carrots, cut into diagonal strips and blanched for 3 minutes
2 ears white corn, shucked, roasted or grilled, and kernels cut from the cobs
Kosher salt and freshly ground black pepper to taste
2 shallots, minced
2 to 3 cloves garlic, minced
1$\frac{1}{2}$ cups Vegetable Stock (see page 203)
$\frac{1}{2}$ cup crème fraîche
Juice of 1 lemon
1 teaspoon minced fresh thyme
1 tablespoon minced fresh basil
3 green onions, white and pale green parts only, cut into very thin rounds

Garnish

Fresh basil leaves
Extra virgin olive oil for drizzling

Place the salmon fillets in a single layer in a shallow dish and season with salt and pepper. Scatter the basil over the top, pressing it into the salmon. Drizzle with a little olive oil, cover with plastic wrap, and refrigerate while you make the ragout and sauce.

Preheat the oven to 400°. Melt the butter in a large sauté pan over medium-high heat, add the blanched vegetables and corn, and sauté until they are just tender, 3 to 4 minutes. Season with salt and pepper. Add the shallots and garlic, and sauté 1 minute more. Add the vegetable stock, crème fraîche, and lemon juice, and simmer until the sauce thickens, 7 to 8 minutes. Stir in the thyme, basil, and half the green onions. Taste and correct the seasoning.

While the sauce cooks, heat the 1 tablespoon olive oil in a large ovenproof sauté pan over medium heat and sauté the salmon, flesh-side down, for 2 minutes. Turn and sauté until the skin is golden brown, about 3 minutes more. Place the fish in the sauté pan in the oven and roast the salmon for 5 minutes, or until it is just slightly transparent in the center.

Using a slotted spoon, divide the ragout among 4 soup plates or pasta bowls. Spoon some of the sauce remaining in the pan over each portion. Place a salmon fillet on top, garnish with basil leaves and a small drizzle of olive oil, and serve immediately.

SERVES 4

Wild Striped Bass with Potatoes, Rapini, and Onion Marmalade

When onions are cooked over low heat for a long time, their natural sugars are released and begin to caramelize; they become rich and luscious, without any intrusive taste of raw onion. Onion marmalade is a scrumptious condiment, excellent not only with this wild bass but with a variety of other foods, from pan-roasted salmon to grilled chicken.

To Drink

Pinot Noir, Zinfandel

Bix recommends: 1999 Seghesio Zinfandel, Sonoma County; 1998 Crocker and Starr Cabernet Franc

Four 6- to 8-ounce wild striped bass fillets
Kosher salt and freshly ground pepper to taste
Extra virgin olive oil for drizzling, plus 1 tablespoon
1 bunch basil, stemmed and cut into fine shreds
$1/_4$ cup olive oil
3 yellow onions, diced
6 cups red port wine
2 cups dry red wine
$1/_2$ cup veal demi-glace (page 210)
1 cup balsamic vinegar
Pinch of sugar (optional)
3 tablespoons dry English mustard
2 tablespoons ice water, plus more as needed
3 tablespoons whole-grain mustard
12 fingerling potatoes
2 tablespoons butter
8 cloves garlic, minced
2 bunches broccoli rabe (rapini), blanched for 2 minutes,
  plunged into ice water, and drained

Place the fish in a shallow dish in a single layer and season with salt and pepper. Drizzle a little olive oil over the fillets and sprinkle with 1 or 2 tablespoons of the basil. Cover with plastic wrap and refrigerate.

To make the marmalade: heat the olive oil in a 3-quart saucepan over low heat, add the onions, and cook, stirring occasionally, until they are very tender, 25 to 30 minutes. Do not let them burn. Season the onions with salt and pepper. Add the port and red wine, increase the heat to medium, and simmer until the liquid is reduced by half. Decrease the heat to low and simmer 10 minutes more. Stir in the demi-glace and balsamic vinegar and continue to simmer until the liquid becomes syrupy.

Taste the onions and add a pinch of sugar if necessary for balance (some onions release more natural sugar than others). Remove the onions from the heat, transfer them to a stainless-steel bowl, and let cool to room temperature.

Meanwhile, put the dry mustard in a small bowl, stir in the ice water to make a thick paste, and add more water as needed to thin the paste to the consistency of prepared mustard. Set aside and stir every 5 minutes for 20 minutes.

Stir the whole-grain mustard into the onions. Taste and correct the seasoning. Stir in the mustard paste and fold in the remaining shredded basil. Cover and set aside at room temperature until ready to serve.

Preheat the oven to 400°. In a medium saucepan of salted boiling water, cook the fingerlings until they are just tender when pierced with a wooden skewer or the tines of a fork. Drain, let cool, cut in half lengthwise, and put in a bowl. Drizzle them with a little olive oil, season with salt and pepper to taste, and spread on a baking sheet in a single layer. Roast the potatoes in the oven, stirring them once or twice, until they are evenly browned, 20 to 25 minutes.

Heat the 1 tablespoon olive oil in a large ovenproof sauté pan over medium heat and cook the bass, flesh-side down, for 2 minutes. Turn and cook until the skin is golden brown, shaking the fish slightly in the pan so that the skin neither sticks nor burns. Transfer the pan to the oven and roast the fish until it is just opaque throughout, about 5 minutes.

Melt the butter in a large sauté pan over medium heat, and sauté the garlic for 30 seconds. Add the broccoli rabe and sauté until tender, 7 to 8 minutes. Season with salt and pepper to taste and remove from the heat.

To serve, spread 2 generous spoonfuls of onion marmalade over the surface of 4 serving plates, using a small rubber spatula or spoon to flatten it into a circle. Divide the fingerlings in rows on top of the marmalade. Scatter the broccoli rabe on top of the potatoes, set a fillet on top of each serving, and add a dollop of marmalade. Drizzle with a little extra virgin olive oil and serve immediately.

SERVES 4

BIZOU

Loretta Keller
Owner and Chef

Before the district south of Market Street became the hip new city scene and long before bistros sprouted on nearly every corner, Loretta Keller opened her diminutive jewelbox of a restaurant, with its disarming warmth and dynamic Mediterranean fare. Keller was voted a Rising Star Chef by *San Francisco Focus* magazine in 1995. Her style is at once down-to-earth and refined, robust yet stylish, and with nary a shred of pretension or culinary foolishness. Her dishes are beautifully presented, but they also make sense as food; you don't have to deconstruct them before you dig in. With the sun-drenched northwestern Mediterranean—that is, eastern Spain, southern France, and northern Italy—as her source of inspiration, of course her seafood creations soar with flavor. You won't find a more satisfying meal anywhere in San Francisco.

598 FOURTH STREET

(415) 543-2222

Mouclade Provençal
(Grilled Mussels with Aioli)

The grill racks of some home barbecues will hold these mussels perfectly, but if the grids on your rack are wide enough for the mussels to slip through, you'll have to improvise or you'll end up with a pile of mussels in the hot ashes. Setting a smaller rack—one used for roasting or broiling in the oven, for example—on top of the grill rack works perfectly. A stovetop grill will not produce the best results, because there will be no smoky flavor from the coals.

$1/_4$ cup olive oil
1 carrot, peeled and finely diced
1 onion, finely diced
2 stalks celery, finely diced
1 teaspoon minced fresh thyme
$1/_2$ teaspoon coarsely ground black pepper
$1/_2$ teaspoon coarsely ground white pepper
$1/_2$ teaspoon coarsely ground and sifted Szechuan peppercorns
1 cup Chicken Stock (page 205)
2 tablespoons minced fresh flat-leaf parsley
4 pounds small black mussels, scrubbed and debearded if necessary
    (see page 220)
Aioli (page 211)
Sea salt to taste
French bread for serving

To Drink

Chardonnay, Marsanne
Bizou recommends: 1998
Manciat-Poncet Macon
Chardonnay, Burgundy

Prepare a fire in a charcoal grill. When the coals are white and have burned down, spread them out and heat the grill rack.

Heat the olive oil in a sauté pan over medium-low heat. Add the carrot, onion, celery, and thyme and cook until soft but not browned, 7 to 8 minutes. Set aside.

Mix the three peppers together and set aside.

Combine the vegetables with the chicken stock and parsley in a large pan (big enough to hold the mussels) over medium heat.

Put the mussels on the grill and cover them with a large metal bowl or lid until they begin to open, 4 to 7 minutes. (The bowl or lid does not need to be tight fitting; the purpose is to catch some of the smoke while the mussels cook.) Sprinkle the mussels generously with the peppercorn mixture and drizzle a bit of olive oil over them. Quickly return the bowl or lid to the grill and cook the mussels without moving them and thereby losing their juices. Using a large, flat spatula, gently remove them from the grill, taking care not to spill their juice, and place them in the pan with the stock. Remove the pan from heat. Using a wooden spoon, toss the liquid and vegetable dice with the mussels and drizzle with about half the aioli. Toss some more until the mussels are coated with the aioli. Transfer to a large serving bowl and sprinkle generously with sea salt. Serve immediately, with French bread and the remaining aioli on the side.

SERVES 8

Sushi in San Francisco

Sushi is one of the finest pleasures available to anyone who loves seafood. To my palate anyway, nothing is better than a slice of buttery *hamachi*, velvety *toro,* or scarlet *maguro,* spiked with a dollop of bold wasabi and a little soy sauce. Cooked fish has its place, of course, and not all species are good raw. But the simple, pristine flavors of expertly prepared sushi and sashimi are unsurpassed; cooking fish that is good raw is always a bit of a compromise.

Sushi and sashimi are more difficult to prepare at home than you might think. The preparation seems simple enough—a little raw fish, a bit of rice, a smear of wasabi—but sushi chefs undergo years of education and intense training, developing and honing the skills that allow them to judge the quality of seafood, understand each species, and prepare it appropriately. I make sashimi only when I find myself with an unexpected bounty of fish that is simply too good to cook, and I never, ever make sushi. It is the one cuisine that I eat for pure pleasure, without a part of me trying to figure out exactly what the chef has done. There are so many excellent sushi restaurants that I never have a problem satisfying a craving for raw fish.

Every neighborhood in San Francisco has a sushi joint of one sort or another. From the Mission district's Blowfish Sushi to Die For, with its televisions tuned to Japanese cartoons and its sound system blasting a techno beat, and the Marina's Ace Wasabi, where traditional and contemporary sushi is served to a young, hip, and loud crowd, to the refined Kyo-ya in the Sheraton Palace Hotel, sushi is available in an environment to suit every sensibility.

If it is tradition and quality you're looking for, you won't do better than at Kyo-ya, long praised for having the finest sushi and sashimi in all of San Francisco. The pricey restaurant is particularly popular with Japanese business travelers, who appreciate the extraordinarily fresh ingredients, expert preparations, and artful presentations. The elegant, almost austere atmosphere enhances rather than eclipses the food. Kyo-ya's chef, Kunihiko Oshikawa, trained in both Osaka and Tokyo, before moving to Oahu, Hawaii. He has been executive chef at Kyo-ya since 1991.

For Americanized sushi, those whimsical combinations and specialty rolls that snake across the plate like fire-breathing dragons, you'll find choices all over the city.

Marinated Anchovies with Heirloom Tomatoes, Preserved Lemons, and Picholine Olives

Anchovies are the only species currently fished commercially in San Francisco Bay, but most of the catch is sold as bait. For fresh anchovies, try specialty stores such as Monterey Fish Market in Berkeley and seafood markets in ethnic communities, such as San Francisco's Chinatown.

6 tablespoons extra virgin olive oil, plus more for drizzling
Juice of 2 lemons, plus more to taste
Sea salt and freshly ground pepper to taste
1 pound fresh anchovies, pan-dressed
4 heirloom tomatoes, cut into wedges
4 ounces picholine olives, pitted and minced
$1/4$ cup fresh flat-leaf parsley leaves
Peel of 2 preserved lemon wedges (see page 215),
   rinsed and finely julienned

To Drink

Riesling, dry Rosé
Bizou recommends: 1998 Nalle Dry Riesling, Cole Ranch, Mendocino County

Combine the 6 tablespoons olive oil and the juice of 2 lemons with the salt and pepper. Pour onto a large platter. Arrange the anchovies on the platter, skin-side up, and let "cure" in the marinade for about 20 minutes, or until the flesh of the fish becomes a bit lighter in color. Turn the fish over and marinate in the refrigerator for 20 minutes. Sprinkle the tomatoes with salt and pepper. Drizzle with olive oil.

Arrange the tomatoes and anchovies on the platter in a random fashion and sprinkle with the olives, parsley leaves, and lemon peel. Sprinkle with lemon juice to taste and drizzle with olive oil.

SERVES 4

Sardine Escalivada with Garbanzo Bean Salad

Escalivada is a Spanish preparation of roast vegetables. In this case, the vegetables are stuffed into the sardines by rolling the fish around the mixture and looping the tail through the fish head to secure the ingredients before baking.

To Drink

Sauvignon Blanc, Trousseau Gris
Bizou recommends: 1998 Poggio
Alle Gazze, Sauvignon Blanc,
Tuscany

1 large artichoke
Olive oil for coating
1 yellow onion, cut into fine julienne
1 fennel bulb, trimmed and cut into fine julienne
Kosher salt and freshly ground black pepper to taste
2 Japanese eggplants, cut into $1/4$ by 1-inch strips
8 fresh sardines, pan-dressed
Extra virgin olive oil for drizzling
Juice of 1 orange
Garbanzo Salad for serving (recipe follows)

Preheat the oven to 400°.

Trim off the base and top 1 inch of the artichoke. With scissors, snap the spines from the leaves. Coat the artichoke with olive oil and place in a roasting pan. Loosely cover with aluminum foil and roast until tender when pierced with a wooden skewer, about 40 minutes. When cool, remove the leaves and choke, cut the heart into very thin slices.

Meanwhile, toss the onion and fennel with a little olive oil, season with salt, and spread out in a small rimmed baking sheet. Loosely cover with aluminum foil and roast in the oven until tender and golden brown, about 25 minutes. Toss the eggplants with a little olive oil, season with salt and pepper, and roast in a separate pan, lightly covered, until they are tender and have released their liquid, about 15 minutes; drain. Combine all the roasted vegetables.

Place the sardines, skin-side down, on a work surface and sprinkle with salt, pepper, olive oil, and the orange juice. Put about 2 teaspoons of the roasted vegetables in the center of each fish. Beginning with the tail, roll the fish up and tuck the tail through the head, securing it in the mouth. Place the stuffed sardines on an oiled or nonstick baking pan and bake for 10 to 12 minutes, or until the sardines are opaque throughout.

Transfer to a serving platter and arrange in a circle. Spoon the salad into the center of the platter. Sprinkle the fish with salt to taste and serve immediately, with the garbanzo salad alongside.

SERVES 4

Garbanzo Salad

Juice of 1 orange
6 tablespoons extra virgin olive oil
Sea salt or kosher salt and freshly ground black pepper to taste
$1/_4$ cup cooked garbanzo beans
$1/_4$ cup fresh flat-leaf parsley leaves
$1/_4$ cup fresh mint leaves
$1/_4$ cup arugula
$1/_4$ cup fresh cilantro leaves (optional)
1 green onion, cut into julienne, white and pale green parts only

In a small bowl, whisk the orange juice and olive oil together. Season with salt and pepper. Toss the garbanzo beans, parsley, mint, arugula, cilantro, and green onions together. Toss the bean mixture with the dressing.

SERVES 4

CHARLES NOB HILL

Ron Siegel
Executive Chef

CHARLES NOB HILL is a 1990s restaurant with an 1890s feel. Refined and elegant, it is the very epitome of civilized pleasure. If you've had any fear that Old World dining might be going the way of the dinosaur and the dial telephone, Charles Nob Hill goes a long way towards alleviating those concerns. A tasting menu includes complex yet logical seafood preparations, and the regular menu gives fish lovers several options, too, including the delicate and refreshing skate wing salad that chef Ron Siegel shares here.

Numerous honors have been bestowed on Ron for his cooking, including three Rising Star Chef awards, from *San Francisco* magazine, the *San Francisco Chronicle,* and *Food and Wine* magazine. Siegel also was the first American to win the Iron Chef competition in Japan, a televised contest in which chefs try to outdo each other in battles that focus on a single ingredient. Ron's battle? Lobster.

The restaurant is located atop Nob Hill. If the fog isn't too heavy after dinner, you might enjoy a walk. The view of the Bay Bridge and the Bay itself is spectacular when the weather cooperates, and there are several elegant bars nearby where a nightcap would be a luxurious conclusion to the evening.

1250 JONES STREET

(415) 771-5400

Nantucket Bay Scallops with Porcini Mushrooms, Osetra Caviar, and Black Truffles

In this recipe, chef Robert Siegel pairs two seductively earthy ingredients—truffles and mushrooms—with the delicate, briny flavors of caviar and scallops for an extraordinarily sophisticated yet fairly simple dish. As is often the case with such dishes, the ingredients are a bit pricey. You can make a more economical version by using golden caviar in place of osetra caviar, and a drizzle of black truffle oil instead of the truffles themselves. It won't be exactly the same, of course, but it will be very good. Fresh porcini mushrooms are usually sold sliced lengthwise and held together by a rubber band; this indicates they have been inspected for the worms that are common in these mushrooms. If you have whole porcinis, be sure to examine them for worms and discard any you find. Spring onions are simply bulb onions (often Spanish Reds) before they've plumped up. If you can't find them in a farmers' market or specialty shop, substitute a small sweet onion, such as a Walla Walla.

5 tablespoons unsalted butter

4 ounces porcini mushrooms, minced

Kosher salt and freshly ground pepper to taste

1 large spring onion, white or red part only, minced

1 cup port wine

24 large Nantucket Bay scallops

3 tablespoons Clarified Butter (page 201)

2 tablespoons osetra caviar

12 fresh chive tips

8 paper-thin slices fresh black truffle

Melt 2 tablespoons of the butter in a small sauté pan over medium-low heat and sauté the mushrooms, stirring occasionally, until limp and tender, 7 to 8 minutes. Season with salt and pepper. Set aside and keep warm. Melt 2 tablespoons of the butter in a small sauté pan over low heat and cook the spring onion, stirring occasionally, until completely tender, 12 to 15 minutes. Season with salt and pepper to taste. Set aside and keep warm.

Pour the port into a small saucepan. Bring to a boil over medium-high heat and cook to reduce to about 2 tablespoons, 10 to 12 minutes. Decrease the heat to low and whisk in the remaining 1 tablespoon butter. Remove from the heat. Set aside and keep warm.

Dry the scallops with a tea towel, and season them on both sides with salt and pepper. Heat the clarified butter in a large sauté pan over high heat and cook the scallops, turning once, until golden brown, 1 to 2 minutes per side.

Arrange 3 large scallop shells or a ramekin on each of 4 individual plates. In one shell on each plate, spoon a little of the port syrup, top it with a spoonful of porcini, and place 2 scallops on top. In another shell on each plate, spoon some of the onion, place 2 scallops on the onion, and add a dollop of caviar on top of the scallops. Add 3 chive tips to each serving of caviar. Place 2 scallops on the third shell of each plate, spoon a little of the cooking juices on top, and top with 2 slices of black truffle. Serve immediately.

SERVES 4

Dungeness Crab Salad
with Citrus Fruits and Avocado

Contrast in taste and texture is the hallmark of this salad, perfect in winter months when both Dungeness crab and citrus are in season. In an unusual flourish, the chef places greens on top of the other ingredients, using them as a garnish rather than as a bed on which the salad is built.

3 tablespoons olive oil

1 large carrot, diced

1 large leek, cleaned and diced

One 2-liter bottle (about 8 cups) dry white wine

1 tablespoon black peppercorns

1 bay leaf

4 cups water

2 large live Dungeness crabs

2 cups freshly squeezed orange juice

Kosher salt and freshly ground black pepper to taste

1 cup extra virgin olive oil, plus more for drizzling

2 limes, peeled and cut into individual sections (see page 218)

3 blood oranges, peeled and cut into individual sections
(see page 218)

2 tangerines, peeled and cut into individual sections (see page 218)

1 grapefruit, peeled and cut into individual sections (see page 218)

1 lemon, peeled and cut into individual sections (see page 218)

2 tablespoons minced fresh chives

1 firm ripe Hass avocado, peeled, pitted, and sliced lengthwise

3 cups mixed salad greens

To Drink

Sauvignon Blanc, Chablis, Soave Classico

Charles Nob Hill recommends:
1997 Monts Mains, Chablis, Premier Cru, François Ravaneau

Heat the 3 tablespoons olive oil in a large pot over medium-low heat and cook the carrot and leek, stirring occasionally, until very tender, 15 to 20 minutes. Add the wine, peppercorns, and bay leaf, increase the heat to high, bring to a boil, and cook until the wine is reduced by half, about 15 minutes. Add the water and return to a boil. Add the crabs and cook for 8 minutes. Remove the crabs from the pot and let cool. Clean and crack the crabs (see page 220). Remove the meat from the shell, and set it aside.

Pour the orange juice into a small nonreactive saucepan and simmer over medium heat until reduced to a thick syrup. Strain through a fine-meshed sieve into a bowl, season with salt and pepper, and gradually whisk in the 1 cup olive oil. Set aside.

Combine the lime, blood orange, tangerine, grapefruit, and lemon segments in a medium bowl and set them aside. Put the crabmeat in a medium bowl, and $1/2$ cup of the orange-flavored oil and the chives, and toss gently but thoroughly. Taste and correct the seasoning.

Divide the avocado slices among 4 individual plates and spoon some of the citrus on top. Spoon the crab on top of the citrus. Scatter the greens on top of each serving, drizzle with a little extra virgin olive oil, and finish by drizzling with some of the remaining orange-flavored oil. Serve immediately.

SERVES 4

Skate Wings with Artichoke Salad
and Caper-Lemon Brown Butter

Artichoke lovers will delight in this dish. It calls for six fresh artichoke hearts, which means there will be all those scrumptious leaves left over. I suggest preparing the artichokes in the morning and enjoying the leaves for lunch (with, perhaps, the aioli on page 211). Yum!

4 skate wing fillets, about 8 ounces each
Kosher salt and freshly ground pepper to taste
Flour for dusting
$1/4$ cup Clarified Butter (see page 201)
6 whole artichoke hearts, cooked until tender
    and finely chopped
2 tablespoons olive oil
2 bunches chives, snipped
2 tablespoons unsalted butter
1 teaspoon freshly squeezed lemon juice
$1/4$ cup Tomato Concassée (page 202)
1 teaspoon capers, minced
2 tablespoons minced fresh flat-leaf parsley

To Drink

Pilsner, lager

Charles Nob Hill recommends:

1997 Kongsgaard, Chardonnay, Napa Valley

Place the skate wing fillets on a work surface and season them on both sides with salt and pepper. Dust with flour. Melt the clarified butter in a large sauté pan over medium heat, add the fish, and cook, turning once, until golden brown, 3 to 4 minutes per side.

Meanwhile, toss the artichoke hearts with the olive oil and chives. Season with salt and pepper to taste. Divide among 4 plates. Place the cooked skate wing fillets on top. Melt the unsalted butter in a clean medium sauté pan over medium heat and cook just until lightly brown; it will be very fragrant. Carefully add the lemon juice, tomato concassée, capers, and parsley. Heat through. Taste and correct the seasoning. Spoon the sauce over the fish and serve immediately.

SERVES 4

CHE

Johnny Alamilla
Executive Chef

Nuevo Latino cuisine has been slow to come to San Francisco (it's been a hit in New York City since the early 1990s), perhaps because the foods of Mexico, Latin America, and South America have been so good and so readily available here for decades. Few chefs seemed compelled to reinvent them until 1999, when Johnny Alamilla became one of the first to offer lusty south-of-the-border creations reinterpreted for contemporary diners who demand more than melt-in-your-mouth carnitas and simple seafood tacos. At Che, you'll find unusual ceviches, seafood salads, and fresh fish presented with all of the refinement of traditional French cuisine, yet with the interplay of explosive flavors found only in warmer climes, all of it served up with live Cuban jazz and a festive atmosphere.

As *San Francisco Seafood* was going to press, Che closed, a casualty of the soaring rents of the South of Market area. Johnny Alamilla plans to reopen his restaurant in early 2001, somewhere in the Mission District. He'll keep fans updated via his website.

WWW.EATATCHE.COM

Black Cod with Roasted Potatoes, Sweet Onions, Pisco Sauce, and Pumpkin Seed Gremolata

Known variously as black cod, sablefish, or butterfish, this member of the skilfish family is unrelated to cod. It is found in the eastern Pacific from Alaska to California, and has rich, moist flesh. Chilean sea bass (which is not really bass) can be substituted for black cod; you can also use snapper fillets of similar size in this recipe. Pisco is a Peruvian liqueur, similar to grappa and with a pleasing orange flavor.

$3/4$ cup ($1^1/_2$ sticks) unsalted butter

1 tablespoon ground coriander

3 sweet onions, such as Peruvian, Vidalia, or Walla Walla, cut into thirds crosswise

3 red onions

Kosher salt and freshly ground pepper to taste

3 tablespoons freshly squeezed orange juice

2 fingerling potatoes, cut in half lengthwise

$1/_3$ cup achiote paste (available in Latino markets), thinned with 2 to 3 tablespoons hot water

1 cup shelled pumpkin seeds, lightly toasted (see page 216)

1 tablespoon minced fresh marjoram

1 tablespoon grated lime zest

1 tablespoon minced fresh flat-leaf parsley

Four 6-ounce boneless black cod fillets

Pisco Sauce (recipe follows)

To Drink

Che recommends: Semillon, Pinot Gris, Sauvignon Blanc

Melt the butter in a large nonreactive pot over medium heat, add the coriander and onions, toss, and season with salt and pepper. Reduce the heat to very low, add the orange juice, cover, and simmer, stirring occasionally, until the onions are very tender, about 1 hour.

Preheat the oven to 350°. Put the potatoes in a large bowl and toss with the achiote paste until they are thoroughly coated. Season with salt and pepper to taste and spread in a single layer on an oiled rimmed baking sheet. Bake until tender, about 45 minutes.

To make the gremolata, chop the toasted pumpkin seeds, put in a small bowl, and toss with the marjoram, lime zest, and parsley. Season with salt and pepper to taste. Set aside.

Increase the oven temperature to 400°. Season the cod fillets on both sides with salt and pepper. Heat a large nonstick ovenproof sauté pan over high heat and sear the fish, skin-side down, until the skin is crisp, 4 to 5 minutes. Turn the fillets over, transfer the pan to the oven, and bake until the fish is opaque throughout but still moist, about 4 minutes.

To serve, place a fish fillet in the center of each of 4 individual plates. Surround each fillet with potatoes and onions. Drizzle with pisco sauce, scatter gremolata on top, and serve immediately.

SERVES 4

Pisco Sauce

1 cup freshly squeezed orange juice
$1/4$ cup pisco
2 shallots, sliced
1 teaspoon coriander seeds
$1/2$ teaspoon lemon juice
2 fresh limes, peeled and all pith removed (see page 218)
1 cup olive oil
Salt and freshly ground pepper to taste

Combine the orange juice, pisco, shallots, and coriander in a small nonreactive saucepan. Bring to a simmer over medium heat and cook until reduced by half. Strain the liquid into a blender or food process. Add the lemon juice and the limes and process until smooth, about 2 minutes. With the machine running, gradually add the olive oil to make a smooth sauce. Season with salt and pepper.

MAKES ABOUT $1 1/2$ CUPS

Sonoran Glazed Prawns with Jicama Salad and Toasted Quinoa

Quinoa is an ancient grain, first cultivated by the Aztecs and today enjoying a resurgence of popularity. Here, it contributes a pleasantly earthy contrast to the bright, tangy flavors of the salad and the sweet heat of the shrimp. Prepare it the day before you serve the dish.

$4^1/_2$ cups water

$1/_2$ cup quinoa

1 tablespoon kosher salt, plus more to taste

1 jicama, peeled and cut into julienne

2 carrots, peeled and cut into julienne

1 English (hothouse) cucumber, peeled, seeded, and cut into julienne

1 red onion, thinly sliced

2 green onions, white and pale green parts only, thinly sliced

$1/_2$ cup plus 1 tablespoon freshly squeezed lime juice

1 teaspoon ground cumin

$1/_4$ cup plus 4 tablespoons olive oil

Freshly ground black pepper to taste

5 plum tomatoes, peeled, seeded, and diced (see page 218)

2 chipotle chiles in adobo sauce, plus 1 teaspoon of the sauce

1 tablespoon honey

1 pound jumbo shrimp, shelled and deveined (see page 219)

To Drink

Riesling, Gewürztraminer

Che recommends: Vinho Verde

In a medium saucepan, bring 4 cups of the water to a boil and stir in the quinoa and the salt. Reduce the heat to low, cover, and cook for 40 minutes. Drain thoroughly and spread the quinoa in a thin layer on a baking sheet. Cover and let dry overnight.

To make the salad, toss the jicama, carrots, cucumber, onion, and green onions with the $1/_2$ cup lime juice, $1/_2$ teaspoon of the cumin, and $1/_4$ cup of the olive oil in a large bowl. Season with salt and pepper and set aside.

To make the glaze, heat 1 tablespoon of the olive oil in a heavy skillet over medium heat, add the tomatoes, and sauté until soft, 10 to 15 minutes. Stir in the chipotle chiles and their sauce and the remaining $1/_2$ cup water. Simmer for 10 minutes. Transfer the mixture to a blender or food processor, add the honey, 1 tablespoon lime juice, and the remaining $1/2$ teaspoon cumin, and process on high until smooth. Pass through a medium-meshed sieve, taste, and season with salt and pepper.

Heat 2 tablespoons of the olive oil in a heavy skillet over medium-high heat, add the quinoa, and fry, tossing frequently, until lightly browned.

Season the prawns on both sides with salt and pepper. Heat the remaining 1 tablespoon olive oil in a large sauté pan over high heat and sauté the prawns for 1 minute. Turn and stir in the glaze. Decrease heat to medium-low and cook until the prawns are evenly pink, about 2 minutes more. Divide the jicama salad among 4 individual serving plates. Top each portion with prawns and a generous spoonful of the cooking liquid. Garnish with fried quinoa and serve immediately.

SERVES 4

Peruvian Ceviche

We usually think of ceviche as fish that has been "cooked" in lemon or lime juice rather than with heat (both acid and heat denature protein, the process that cooking describes), but this recipe shows another style of preparing ceviche. No matter what the method used for preparing the fish, tangy citrus flavors are characteristic of all ceviches.

Court Bouillon (recipe follows; see also note, below)
1 pound calamari, cleaned and sliced into rings
    (see page 219)
8 ounces baby octopus, cleaned and quartered, or
    more calamari
16 to 20 black mussels, scrubbed and debearded
    if necessary (see page 220)
1 teaspoon minced garlic
3 tablespoons olive oil
6 shallots, minced
1 Fresno or Anaheim chile, seeded and diced
2 bay leaves
1 cup dry white wine
2 cups Fish Fumet (page 207)
$1/4$ cup squid ink (see note, next page)
$1/4$ cup freshly squeezed lemon juice
$1/4$ cup freshly squeezed lime juice
Salt and freshly ground pepper to taste
1 cup diced Yukon Gold potatoes (3 or 4), boiled
1 tablespoon minced fresh cilantro for garnish

To Drink

Lager, Riesling, Gewürztraminer
Che recommends: Torrontés
Riojano, Argentina

Put the court bouillon in a medium pot and bring to a simmer over medium-low heat. Add the calamari and octopus and poach for just 90 seconds. Drain, reserving the poaching liquid. Plunge the calamari and octopus into ice water for 1 minute. Drain thoroughly and set aside.

Pour about $1/3$ cup of the court bouillon into a large sauté pan and bring to a simmer over medium-low heat. Add the mussels and garlic, cover, and steam until the mussels have just opened, 7 to 8 minutes. Transfer the mussels to a bowl and discard any that have not opened. Heat the olive oil in the same sauté pan over medium heat and sauté the shallots and chile until limp, 4 to 5 minutes. Add the bay leaves and wine and simmer until the wine is reduced by half. Stir in the fish fumet and squid ink.

Decrease the heat to low and simmer for 30 minutes. Stir in the lemon and lime juices, season with salt and pepper, and remove from the heat.

Combine the calamari, octopus, mussels, and potatoes in a large shallow serving bowl and toss gently with the fumet mixture. Taste, season with salt and pepper, and garnish with cilantro. Chill thoroughly before serving.

SERVES 4

Court Bouillon

2 white onions, coarsely chopped
1 head celery, coarsely chopped
2 bay leaves
1 cup dry white wine
$^1/_2$ cup freshly squeezed lemon juice
1 teaspoon black peppercorns
3 cups cold water

Combine all of the ingredients in a large nonreactive saucepan. Bring to a boil over high heat, reduce the heat to low, and barely simmer for 30 minutes. Strain into a clean saucepan.

MAKES ABOUT 4 CUPS

Notes: Squid ink is available in Japanese and other Asian markets, and occasionally in Italian markets.

The court bouillon can be strained and used again to poach fish or shellfish. Store it in the refrigerator for 3 to 4 days, or in the freezer for up to 2 months.

ELISABETH DANIEL

Daniel Patterson
Co-owner and Executive Chef

For the nearly six years that Babette's Restaurant and Wine Bar reigned on the historic square in downtown Sonoma, an hour north of San Francisco, it was unsurpassed, with eloquent dishes shaped by the obsessive creativity and extraordinary talent of its chef, Daniel Patterson. In 1997, Patterson was named one of America's top ten new chefs by *Food and Wine* magazine, the same year he received the Rising Star Chef award from *San Francisco* magazine. Shortly after Babette's received a glowing review in *Gourmet* magazine, it closed. Patterson and his wife, Elisabeth Ramsey, wanted a larger audience, and they have found it on the edge of the Financial District. Elisabeth Daniel is a sophisticated oasis where guests linger over the slow progression of six-course prix-fixe dinners. There is always a seafood course, as well as other seafood selections, such as Patterson's renowned rare ahi tuna suspended in a golden gelée of lemon and black pepper, among the first-course offerings. One of his best-known dishes is an ethereal chive mousse, served in a pristine eggshell and topped with a mound of briny beluga caviar. Although both a command of classic French techniques and an extremely sensitive palate are crucial elements of Patterson's style, flawless ingredients are central to his success.

550 Washington Street

(415) 397-6129

Salt-Cured Sardines with Fennel and Tapenade

Chef Daniel Patterson makes thin olive oil crackers to serve with these cured sardines as an *amuse-bouche*, presented to all of Elisabeth Daniel's customers after they have ordered. To serve at home, choose the thinnest cracker you can find.

To Drink

Champagne
Elisabeth Daniel recommends:
Billecart Salmon "Brut Reserve"
N.V.

6 sardine fillets

Sel gris, ground, or kosher salt to taste

About $^3/_4$ cup fruity, green olive oil

Marinated Fennel (recipe follows)

Thin crackers for serving

Tapenade (recipe follows)

2 tablespoons snipped fresh chives

Arrange the sardine fillets, skin-side down, in a single layer in a shallow dish. Sprinkle each fillet with sel gris. Cover the dish tightly with plastic wrap and refrigerate overnight.

Remove the sardines from the dish, pat them dry, and stack them, flesh-side down, in a small container. Add olive oil to cover the sardines. Cover tightly and refrigerate for at least 24 hours or up to two weeks.

To assemble, drain the sardines thoroughly and cut them into $^1/_2$-inch-wide diagonal slices. Spoon a small amount of fennel onto each cracker, place a slice of sardine on the fennel, and top with a small dollop of tapenade. Sprinkle with chives and serve immediately.

SERVES 6

Tapenade

....

2 tablespoons minced pitted niçoise olives
2 tablespoons minced pitted picholine olives
2 thin slices garlic, minced
3 fresh rosemary leaves, minced
Leaves from $1/2$ small thyme sprig, minced
3 fresh flat-leaf parsley leaves, minced
$1/4$ teaspoon red wine vinegar
$3/4$ teaspoon fruity extra virgin olive oil
1 teaspoon capers, minced
Freshly ground pepper to taste

In a small bowl, toss together the olives, garlic, rosemary, thyme, parsley, vinegar, olive oil, and capers. Season with pepper and set aside. Use now, or cover and refrigerate for up to 1 week.

MAKES $1/4$ CUP

Marinated Fennel

....

$1/4$ cup shaved and chopped fennel
$1 1/2$ teaspoons crème fraîche
$1/2$ teaspoon red wine vinegar
$1/2$ teaspoon freshly squeezed lemon juice
$1/2$ teaspoon fruity extra virgin olive oil
Sel gris, ground, or kosher salt to taste
Freshly ground black pepper to taste

In a small bowl, toss together the fennel, crème fraîche, vinegar, lemon juice, and olive oil. Season with salt and pepper. Cover tightly with plastic wrap, and refrigerate for up to 3 hours.

MAKES ABOUT $1/4$ CUP

Oyster Mousse with Sorrel Coulis and Sevruga Caviar

It can be difficult to adapt a chef's recipe for the home cook, in part because restaurant chefs prepare larger quantities than we do at home. In this recipe, you'll need to prepare a little more of the egg mixture than you will need because you cannot get a proper consistency with less.

To Drink

Sancerre, Chenin Blanc

Elisabeth Daniel recommends:

1995 Francois Raveneau Chablis "Butteaux"

2 teaspoons unsalted butter

1 shallot, thinly sliced

Guisto's fine sea salt, finely ground sel gris, or kosher salt to taste

2 tablespoons dry white wine

$1/4$ cup heavy whipping cream

$1 1/2$ teaspoons plain gelatin

4 ounces fresh shucked oysters (15 to 25 oysters), preferably
   Hog Island Sweetwaters or Fanny Bays (liquor reserved)

1 egg

1 egg yolk

Freshly ground white pepper to taste

Sorrel Coulis (recipe follows)

$1 1/2$ ounces sevruga caviar

Melt the butter in a small sauté pan over low heat, add the shallot, season with a little salt, and cook slowly until tender, about 12 minutes. Increase the heat to medium, add the wine, and simmer until the wine is reduced by half, 3 to 4 minutes. Add the cream and simmer until it is reduced by half, 5 to 6 minutes. Add the gelatin and whisk until it dissolves. Add the oysters and oyster liquor, remove from the heat, and stir gently.

Using a heavy-duty mixer, beat the egg and egg yolk on high speed until pale and thick. Meanwhile, put the oyster mixture in a food processor and process for 7 seconds. Strain the purée into a stainless-steel bowl set over a bowl of ice. Stir constantly with a rubber spatula until the mixture thickens. Remove the bowl from the ice.

Fold half of the egg mixture into the oyster mixture (reserve the remaining egg mixture for another use). Season with salt and pepper. Set the bowl over the ice and stir gently until the mixture begins to set. Pour the mousse into a small container. Cover and refrigerate for at least 1 hour or up to 8 hours.

To serve, ladle about 2 tablespoons of the coulis into a shallow bowl about 5 inches in diameter. Use a large soup spoon to form an oval-shaped quenelle of mousse in the center of the sauce. Top the mousse with a thin line of caviar down the center and serve immediately.

SERVES 8 TO 10

Note: Oyster liquor is the liquid inside the shell with the oyster. To reserve the liquor, shuck the oysters over a bowl, and then pass the liquid through a cheesecloth to remove any shell or sand. Rinse the oysters in cool water to remove any shell particles, and drain them thoroughly. If you have the oysters shucked at the fish market, ask that the liquid be reserved for you and be sure to strain it before using it.

Sorrel Coulis

1 teaspoon unsalted butter
1 shallot, thinly sliced
Guisto's fine sea salt, finely ground sel gris, or kosher salt to taste
$^{1}/_{2}$ cup heavy whipping cream
$^{1}/_{2}$ cup water
3 bunches sorrel (2 to 3 cups, loosely packed), stemmed and
    coarsely chopped
1 tablespoon crème fraîche
Freshly ground pepper to taste

Melt the butter in a sauté pan over low heat. Add the shallot, season with a little salt, and cook until very tender, about 12 minutes. Increase the heat to medium-low, add the cream and water, and simmer for 20 minutes. Remove from the heat and let cool slightly.

Put the sorrel in a blender and pulse while pouring in the shallot cream. Continue to blend until the mixture is uniformly green. Add the crème fraîche and pulse to incorporate. Pass the mixture through a fine-meshed sieve. Taste and correct the seasoning with salt and white pepper.

MAKES ABOUT 1 CUP

Arctic Char with Ragout of Spring Onions, Green Garlic, and Fava Beans

Nearly all commercially available Arctic char is farm raised. It is closely related to the Dolly Varden trout, and its flesh ranges in color from pale pink to deep red. Char has a mild flavor and a moderate amount of fat, and is ideal with this delicate spring ragout.

To Drink

Viognier, Semillon

Elisabeth Daniel recommends:

1999 Calera Viognier Mt. Harlan

1 tablespoon unsalted butter

3 stalks green garlic, including pale green parts,
    cut into thin rounds

Sel gris, ground, or kosher salt to taste

2 cups julienned spring onions

Freshly ground pepper to taste

1 1/2 pounds fava beans, shelled (1 1/2 cups),
    blanched for 1 minute and peeled

2 tablespoons Vegetable Stock (page 203)

1 tablespoon minced fresh chervil

1 tablespoon olive oil

6 Arctic char fillets

Sherry Vinegar Sabayon (recipe follows)

Melt 1/2 tablespoon of the butter in a small, heavy saucepan over low heat and add the green garlic and salt. Sauté the garlic for 3 to 4 minutes, or until it begins to soften. Add the onions, season again with salt, and cook, stirring occasionally, until both the onions and garlic are very tender, 20 to 25 minutes.

Line a baking sheet with parchment paper. Taste and correct the seasoning of the onion mixture with salt and pepper. Spread the mixture on the prepared pan to cool, reserving 1 tablespoon to use in the sabayon.

Melt the remaining 1/2 tablespoon butter in a small saucepan over medium-low heat. Add the fava beans and vegetable stock. Simmer until the fava beans are just tender, about 2 minutes. Add the onion mixture and cook for 2 or 3 minutes. Stir in the chervil. Taste and correct for seasonings.

Heat the olive oil in a large nonstick sauté pan over medium heat. Season the char fillets on both sides with salt and pepper to taste and sauté until lightly browned on each side, 2 to 3 minutes per side.

Divide the vegetable ragout evenly among 6 warmed plates, spoon the sabayon around the vegetables, and set a fillet on top of each portion. Serve immediately.

SERVES 6

Sherry Vinegar Sabayon

....

$1/_4$ cup Vegetable Stock (page 203)
1 tablespoon onion-garlic mixture (from the ragout, opposite)
1 tablespoon sherry vinegar
Pinch of salt
1 large egg, lightly beaten
1 tablespoon fruity extra virgin olive oil

Heat the vegetable stock and onion-garlic mixture in a small saucepan and when it is hot, remove it from the heat, cover the pan, and let steep for 15 minutes. Strain the mixture through a fine-meshed sieve and add the sherry vinegar and salt. Set aside.

Combine the egg and the vegetable stock mixture in a heavy saucepan. Heat over medium-low heat, whisking vigorously and turning the pot constantly to prevent hot spots, until the mixture is thickened and pale. Remove from the heat and whisk in the olive oil. Taste and correct the seasonings. Serve immediately.

MAKES ABOUT $2/_3$ CUP

FARALLON

Mark Franz
Executive Chef

Farallon, just off Union Square, is an enchanting reverie, an opulent aquatic fantasyland for adults. If you are willing to suspend disbelief, you will be dazzled by the beguiling interior, where every element seems to echo the sea's bewitching garden of creatures and plants. Overhead, jellyfish chandeliers, their handblown glass tentacles aglow, further the illusion that you are underwater. Fixtures everywhere do double duty: A copper hood evokes fish scales; sconces resemble barnacles and coral; a pale, circular room feels like the inside of a scallop shell; a curving staircase is embedded with thousands of tiny beads that resemble plump jewels of caviar. There are sea urchin chandeliers and wavelike walls and windows. The environment is utterly captivating, and the cuisine of Mark Franz mirrors the whimsical decor: A pyramid of seafood gelée with suspended morsels of shrimp, scallops, and lobster is a signature dish. If you love seafood, you will find Farallon, named for the chain of islands just off the coast, irresistible. And although this downtown attraction is sophisticated enough to please adults, it is also a friendly, appealing place to take children.

450 Post Street
(415) 956-6969

Grilled Abalone with Yuzu Gribiche Sauce

Yuzu is a yellow Japanese fruit that resembles a tangerine in size and shape but has a unique flavor and aroma. The juice is extremely tart and the zest very aromatic. Yuzu is not available fresh in the United States, but you can sometimes find small jars of the juice in Japanese markets. Use lime or lemon juice as a substitute if you can't find yuzu juice.

Six 4- to 6-inch live abalone
Leaves from 6 sprigs thyme, minced
2 cups olive oil
Kosher salt and freshly ground pepper to taste
1 clove garlic, minced
1 anchovy fillet, minced
2 tablespoons yuzu juice or freshly squeezed lime
**   or lemon juice, plus more to taste**
3 hard-cooked eggs, cut in half
1 egg yolk
2 tablespoons warm water
2 tablespoons minced cornichons
2 tablespoons capers, minced
12 fresh chives, minced
Leaves from 6 sprigs tarragon, minced

To Drink

Sauvignon Blanc
Farallon recommends: 1999 Isabel
Sauvignon Blanc, New Zealand;
1998 Araujo Sauvignon Blanc,
Eisele Vineyard, Napa Valley

Pry the abalone meat out of the shell and set it aside. Scrub the shells, rinse them thoroughly, and set them aside. Discard the abalone viscera and trim away the dark mantle on the edges of the shellfish. Using a very sharp knife, slice the abalone lengthwise into very thin disks ($1/8$ to $1/4$ inch thick). Place each slice on a clean cutting board and gently pound it with a rolling pin or meat mallet just enough to soften the meat and release its fragrant white juice. Put the pounded abalone in a shallow glass bowl. Toss the abalone with the thyme and $1/2$ cup of the olive oil. Season with salt and pepper, cover, and marinate for 1 hour.

Meanwhile, make the sauce. Combine the garlic, anchovy, and yuzu juice in a small bowl and season with salt and pepper to taste. Separate the cooked egg whites from the yolks and mince each, keeping them separate. Add the cooked egg yolks, raw egg yolk, and warm water to the garlic mixture and mix thoroughly. Gradually whisk in the remaining $1\frac{1}{2}$ cups olive oil to make an emulsified mixture. Fold in the cornichons, capers, chives, and tarragon. Taste and correct the seasoning. Set the sauce aside.

Prepare a fire in a charcoal grill or heat a stovetop grill pan over high heat. Grill each piece of abalone for about 30 seconds, then turn and grill 30 seconds more. When all of the abalone has been grilled, use a large, sharp knife to cut it into medium julienne. Fill each reserved shell with abalone meat, top with a generous spoonful of sauce, and serve immediately.

SERVES 6

Poached Oysters and Potato Gnocchi
with Champagne Sabayon
and Tarragon Cucumbers

If you visit the Bay Area and have time for a drive to the Marin County coast, try to stop by Hog Island Shellfish Company in Marshall. You'll need to bring your own bread and wine, but they'll sell you the oysters and loan you a shucking glove and knife—they'll even teach you how to use it. They also have a picnic area and kettle grills, if you prefer your oysters grilled.

Gnocchi

1 $\frac{1}{4}$ pounds (about 2 large) russet potatoes
2 egg yolks
1 teaspoon kosher salt
$\frac{1}{4}$ teaspoon freshly ground pepper
1 cup unbleached all-purpose flour, plus more as needed

To Drink
Dry Champagne
Farallon recommends: 1990
Bollinger Grande Année; 1993
Roederer Estate, L'Ermitage,
Anderson Valley

Cucumbers

2 English (hothouse) cucumbers, peeled, seeded, and cut into fine julienne
Leaves from 6 sprigs tarragon, minced
$\frac{1}{4}$ cup rice vinegar
Kosher salt and freshly ground pepper to taste

Sauce

4 egg yolks
$\frac{1}{2}$ cup dry champagne
$\frac{1}{4}$ cup water
Kosher salt and freshly ground pepper to taste

2 cups Fish Fumet (page 207)
2 cups dry champagne
20 Hog Island Sweetwater oysters, shucked (liquor reserved)
6 sprigs tarragon for garnish

To make the gnocchi, preheat the oven to 375°. Bake the potatoes until they are tender when pierced with a knife, about 45 minutes. Lower the oven temperature to 250°. Let the potatoes cool to the touch. Scoop out the flesh, place it on a baking sheet, and dry it in the oven for about 10 minutes. Press the potato flesh through a potato ricer onto a clean work surface. In a small bowl, whisk the egg yolks with the salt and pepper. Add the potatoes and mix thoroughly. On a floured board, knead until the dough begins to come together. Add $3/4$ cup of the flour and continue to knead for about 2 minutes, or until soft, malleable, and slightly sticky. If the dough seems too sticky, knead in the remaining $1/4$ cup of flour. Do not knead the dough for longer than 4 minutes, or it may become too dry.

Break off one-quarter of the dough. Roll it into a cigar-shaped log about $3/4$ inch in diameter and cut the log into $1/2$-inch pieces. In a small pot of salted boiling water, cook 2 gnocchi until they rise to the surface, about 2 minutes. Cook 2 minutes more and use a slotted spoon to transfer them to a plate. If the gnocchi fall apart in the water, knead an additional 2 tablespoons of flour into the dough. Prepare the rest of the gnocchi, set them on a baking sheet dusted with flour, cover with plastic wrap, and refrigerate while preparing the rest of the recipe or for up to 8 hours.

To prepare the cucumbers, put them in a bowl and toss with the tarragon and vinegar. Season with salt and pepper, cover with plastic wrap, and refrigerate until ready to serve.

To make the sauce, fill a medium pot half full with water, bring it to a boil and decrease the heat so that the water just simmers. Combine the egg yolks, the $1/2$ cup champagne, and the water in a metal bowl that will fit on top of the pan of simmering water. Place it over the pan and whisk the mixture constantly until it is frothy and slightly thickened. Remove the bowl from the heat immediately and season the mixture lightly with salt and pepper. (If it looks like scrambled eggs, it is overcooked and you will need to begin again with fresh ingredients.) Set aside and keep warm over tepid water.

Combine the fish fumet and the 2 cups champagne in a medium saucepan and bring to a simmer. Fill a larger pot two-thirds full with water and bring it to a boil. Salt generously and reduce the heat to a rapid simmer.

Cook the gnocchi in the pot of simmering water until they float to the surface. Cook 30 seconds more and use a slotted spoon to transfer them to a colander.

When the gnocchi float to the surface, season the fumet with salt and pepper, drop the shucked oysters and the reserved liquor into the simmering stock, and poach the oysters for about 30 seconds, or until they plump and their edges begin to curl. Using a slotted spoon, transfer the oysters to a strainer.

Working quickly, divide the gnocchi among warmed bowls and top each portion with 4 or 5 oysters. Spoon some of the warm sauce over the oysters and gnocchi. Place some of the cucumbers alongside each portion and garnish with a sprig of tarragon. Serve immediately.

SERVES 4 TO 6

R These Oysters Okay?

Growing up in the Bay Area, I learned early not to eat shellfish during months that didn't include an "r," which is to say from May through August. I heard countless horror stories about what would happen if I did, and most involved painful death. As proved true with many such admonitions of childhood, the reality was slightly different. Still, it's not a bad rule to avoid eating shellfish—especially mollusks—during the warm months. When the temperature of seawater rises, oysters spawn, creating a milky white substance known as milt, an oyster's invest-ment in its future. The milt won't harm you, but if you have a sensitive palate, it might gross you out. Oysters in this stage of their cycle are unpleasant when eaten raw; even large ones can be yucky if they are too milty, though smaller oysters are just fine barbecued. If your preference is for lean, briny, meaty oysters, it is probably best to savor them in the colder months, before they begin making their milt. In the 1990s, a new genetic strain known as the triploid oyster appeared; this sterile shellfish never spawns and therefore never becomes milty or soft.

Seared Rockfish with Pea Ravioli, Dungeness Crab, and Mint Pesto

To Drink

Pinot Noir

Farallon recommends: 1997
Littorai Pinot Noir Hirsch Vineyard,
Sonoma Coast; 1996 Louis Jadot
Savign-les-Beaune Les Dominode

If you're pressed for time or simply don't feel like making raviolis, you can serve this dish with just the mint pesto and crab. The delicious raviolis elevate the dish to what we expect from top restaurants such as Farallon, but they are not absolutely essential when you're preparing the fish at home. Farallon's rockfish and rock cod are provided by two local fishermen who catch it near the Duxberry Reef, just off the coast of Bolinas in Marin County.

Ravioli

2 tablespoons unsalted butter
1 pound English peas, shelled (1 cup)
1 teaspoon minced fresh tarragon
Salt and freshly ground pepper to taste
32 wonton wrappers

Mint Pesto

$3/4$ cup loosely packed fresh
    mint leaves
$1/4$ cup loosely packed fresh
    flat-leaf parsley leaves
$1/4$ cup extra virgin olive oil
1 tablespoon pine nuts
$1/2$ teaspoon freshly squeezed lemon juice
Salt and freshly ground pepper to taste

Butter Sauce

$1/4$ cup Fish Fumet (page 207)
$1/4$ cup dry white wine
$1/2$ cup (1 stick) unsalted butter, chilled, cut into tablespoon-sized pieces
Salt and freshly ground pepper to taste

Rockfish

Four 6-ounce rockfish fillets, bones removed
Kosher salt and freshly ground pepper to taste
$1/4$ cup olive oil
1 cup fresh lump Dungeness crabmeat, picked over for shells

To make the ravioli, melt the butter over medium heat in a small saucepan and cook the peas for 3 minutes, or until they are slightly softened. Add the tarragon, season with salt and pepper, and purée in a blender or food processor. Let cool.

To assemble, lay 16 of the wonton wrappers on a work surface. Place 1 heaping tea-spoonful of pea purée in the center of each wrapper. Brush the edges of the wrapper with water, top each one with a second wrapper, and firmly press the edges together to seal them, creating a small mound in the center as you push out as much air as possible from the ravioli. Using a 3-inch round or scalloped biscuit or cookie cutter, cut out the raviolis and place them on a parchment-lined baking sheet that has been lightly sprinkled with flour. Store, uncovered, in the refrigerator for up to 8 hours.

To make the pesto, blanch the mint and parsley in boiling water for about 10 sec-onds. Drain and plunge the herbs into a bowl of cold water to set the color. Using your hands, squeeze out as much moisture as possible. Combine in a blender or food processor with 2 tablespoons of the olive oil and purée, scraping the sides of the con-tainer once. With the machine running, gradually add the remaining olive oil. Add the pine nuts and lemon juice, and pulse for a few seconds until the mixture forms a smooth sauce. Season with salt and pepper, transfer to a small container, and press a piece of plastic wrap onto the surface of the pesto. Set aside.

Preheat the oven to 375°. Bring a large pot of water to a rapid simmer and salt gen-erously.

To make the sauce, in a small saucepan, bring the fish fumet and white wine to a boil and cook to reduce the liquid by half. Decrease heat to very low. Whisk in the butter, 2 tablespoons at a time, whisking after each addition until the sauce thickens and emulsifies before adding more. Season with salt and pepper. Keep the sauce warm over tepid water. Whisk occasionally so that the sauce does not separate.

Season the fish fillets with salt and pepper. Heat a large, ovenproof skillet over medium-high heat. Add the olive oil to the skillet, heat for a few seconds, and place the rockfish, skin-side down, in the pan. Cook for 4 minutes, or until the skin is crisp and golden brown. Using a slotted spatula, gently turn the fillets over and transfer the skillet to the oven for 5 minutes, or until opaque throughout.

Meanwhile, cook the ravioli in the pot of rapidly simmering water for 3 minutes. Check for doneness by cutting off a small edge of 1 ravioli and biting into it to see if the wonton wrapper is tender. If tender, use a large, flat strainer to transfer the ravioli to a bowl; if not, cook 30 to 45 seconds longer. Add 1 tablespoonful or so of the butter sauce to the bowl and carefully toss the ravioli to coat them.

Put the crabmeat in a small bowl and toss with some of the butter sauce. Arrange 4 ravioli on each of 4 warmed dinner plates. Spoon a little of the remaining butter sauce over each portion. Set the fish fillets, skin-side up, on top of the ravioli, drizzle with some of the mint pesto, and top with the crabmeat. Serve immediately, with the remaining mint pesto on the side.

SERVES 4

The Farallon Islands

On a clear day, when the wind is up and the fog is nowhere to be found, you can just see the Farallon Islands shimmering on the horizon, mirage-like, off the Golden Gate. This seven-island chain, the name of which means "small rocky islands," has been a protected bird sanctuary for nearly a century and a lighthouse was built here in 1855. The islands are part of the City and County of San Francisco.

The Oceanic Society offers excursions to the islands. Visitors are not allowed off the boat, but the view from the small bay is captivating (and the initially overpowering aroma of bird guano recedes after a few minutes). Sea lions lounge on the beach, birds reel and soar overhead, and at the right time of year you might spot migrating whales. I once saw two blue whales, the earth's largest mammals, frolicking just north of the islands.

FIFTH FLOOR

George Morrone
Executive Chef

F EW RESTAURANTS ANYWHERE have drawn the instant accolades that have been bestowed on Fifth Floor, where George Morrone's creations have dazzled even the most jaded professional palates. The world recedes as you wind your way through the Palomar Hotel to the restaurant's clubby interior, where rich dark woods and zebra-striped carpets suggest venison, boar, and other wild game. Yet seafood shimmers in the hands of this young chef. At Aqua, Morrone dazzled fans with his seafood couscous and tuna with foie gras. Here, Ocean Delicacies is one of the most lauded dishes: Nestled in a large plate are four smaller plates, one with gingery sea urchin flan; one with a salmon paillard with lemon vinaigrette and clams; another holding a Belon oyster baked on a bed of cipollini onions and red wine butter sauce; and finally, a sea scallop on a bed of potato purée topped with beurre blanc and caviar. The memorable, sophisticated, yet entirely logical creations of Fifth Floor are about as far from the earthy simplicity of cracked Dungeness crab at Swan Oyster Depot or a bowl of steamers at the Old Clam House as it's possible to get. Both styles have their place, but if you're looking to be dazzled, you won't do better than here.

12 FOURTH STREET

(415) 348-1555

Oyster Bisque with Leek Flan

When it is heated, cream expands rapidly in volume, so be sure to use a large saucepan so it doesn't boil over. This elegant soup serves eight, making it ideal for a dinner party. I'd follow it with a simple, bright main course, such as the petrale sole on page 33, the baked rock cod on page 177, or Tadich Grill's Pan-Fried Sand Dabs on page 194.

To Drink
Chenin Blanc
Fifth Floor recommends: 1997
Domaine des Baumard
Savennieres Trie Speciale

Leek Flan

1 tablespoon kosher salt, plus more to taste

8 ounces leeks, including pale green parts, diced

$3/4$ cup heavy whipping cream

$3/4$ cup milk

1 egg

1 egg yolk

Freshly ground white pepper to taste

Oyster Bisque

8 cups heavy whipping cream

2 tablespoons olive oil

2 white onions, sliced

20 large oysters, shucked (liquor reserved)

$2 1/2$ cups dry champagne

Kosher salt to taste

Cayenne pepper to taste

2 shallots, minced

Pinch of saffron threads

$1 1/2$ cups dry champagne

16 small oysters, such as Hog Island Sweetwaters, shucked

2 tablespoons freshly grated horseradish or minced fresh chives for garnish

To make the flan, preheat the oven to 250°. Butter eight 2-ounce custard cups. Fill a medium saucepan two-thirds full with water, add the 1 tablespoon salt, and bring to a boil over high heat. Decrease the heat to medium, add the leeks, and simmer until they are tender, 8 to 10 minutes. Drain thoroughly. Return the leeks to the saucepan, add the cream and milk, and bring to a boil over medium heat. Pour the leek mixture into a blender and purée until smooth. Strain through a fine-meshed sieve into a medium bowl, pressing on the back of the solids with a large spoon. In a small bowl, whisk the egg and egg yolk together. Whisk the egg mixture into the leek purée. Season with salt and pepper.

Pour the flan mixture into the custard cups, filling each one three-quarters full. Set the cups in a baking dish. Carefully add boiling water to the baking dish to come halfway up the sides of the cups. Bake until the flan is firm and just begins to pull away from the sides of the cups, 15 to 20 minutes. Remove from the oven. Set aside and keep warm.

Meanwhile, to make the bisque, pour the cream into a large saucepan. Bring to simmer over medium-high heat and cook until it is reduced by half, about 20 minutes. Set aside.

Heat the olive oil in a medium, heavy saucepan over low heat. Add the onions and cook slowly until they are very tender, about 20 minutes. Increase the heat to medium, add the large oysters and their liquor, and cook until the oysters plump, about 3 minutes. Add $1^1/_2$ cups of the champagne and bring to a boil. Add the reduced cream and bring to a boil again. Season with salt and cayenne. Strain the soup through a fine-meshed sieve, pressing on the oysters and onions with the back of a large spoon to extract as much liquid as possible. Pour the strained soup into a clean saucepan. Set aside and keep warm.

Put the shallots in a small saucepan, add the saffron, and the remaining 1 cup champagne. Bring to a simmer and cook until the liquid is almost entirely evaporated. Working in batches, purée the soup and shallot reduction in a blender until smooth. Strain through a fine-meshed sieve. Return the soup to a clean saucepan.

To serve, heat the soup over medium heat until it boils. Meanwhile, bring the $1^1/_2$ cups of champagne to a boil in a medium saucepan, add the small oysters and poach for $1^1/_2$ minutes, or until plump. Drain the oysters. Unmold a flan into each of 8 warmed shallow soup bowls and ladle the bisque around the flan. Top each flan with 2 poached oysters and garnish with the horseradish or chives. Serve immediately.

SERVES 8

Seared Sea Scallops with Fennel
Orange Salad and Balsamic Vinegar

Watermelon radishes range in size from that of a Ping-Pong ball to that of a tennis ball; the smaller ones are best. You can find these beautiful radishes—green on the outside with marbled pink interiors—in specialty stores and farmers' markets. True balsamic vinegar —*aceto balsamico tradizionale*— is as thick as syrup, nearly as sweet, and extraordinarily complex. It is also very expensive ($100 or more for a 3.3-ounce bottle), in part because it is aged for so long—at least twenty years and often longer. Ten-year-old balsamic vinegar shares some of the characteristics of the real thing, and costs much less.

1 small watermelon radish, shaved paper thin

1 small black radish, shaved paper thin

4 tablespoons orange-infused olive oil (see note, opposite)

Kosher salt and freshly ground pepper to taste

$1/_2$ cup mixed fresh herb leaves, such as basil, tarragon, chives, and parsley, minced

Zest of 2 oranges, minced

1 teaspoon pink peppercorns

1 fennel bulb, trimmed and shaved paper thin

2 oranges, peeled and cut into segments (see page 218)

8 large sea scallops

2 tablespoons olive oil

2 tablespoons 10-year-old balsamic vinegar

In the center of each of 4 dinner plates, overlap 2 slices of watermelon radish with 2 slices of black radish. Drizzle each serving with 1 tablespoon of the orange-infused olive oil and season with salt and pepper. Sprinkle with half of the herbs and half of the orange zest. Lightly crush the pink peppercorns and sprinkle over the radishes and herbs.

In a bowl, toss together the fennel, the remaining herbs, the remaining zest, and the orange segments. Drizzle the remaining 3 tablespoons orange-infused olive oil over the mixture, toss lightly, and season with salt and pepper. Spoon some of the salad on each plate, placing it on top of the radishes.

Season the scallops on both sides with salt and pepper. Heat the 2 tablespoons olive oil in a sauté pan over high heat, add the scallops, and cook for 1 to 2 minutes on each side, or until they are golden brown on both sides and just becoming firm to the touch. Transfer the scallops to a plate and let rest for 1 minute. Divide the scallops among the servings, placing one on each side of the salad. Drizzle each serving with some of the balsamic vinegar and serve immediately.

SERVES 4

Note: There are several brands of orange-infused olive oil on the market today. I recommend O, made using organic blood oranges and ripe mission olives.

How a San Francisco Chef Rescued the Abalone from Certain Oblivion

The States Restaurant, once located not far from where Fifth Floor is today, thrived in San Francisco from 1907 until the advent of the Volstead Act, which ushered in Prohibition. According to *Sumptuous Dining in Gaslight San Francisco,* it was States' chef, "Pop" Ernst, who first pounded an abalone into submissive tastiness. Without proper tenderizing, abalone is tough and chewy, nearly inedible. Ernst figured this out, then dredged the softened muscle in flour and eggs, fried it, and dazzled his customers. The abalone quickly became a delicacy.

Roasted Monkfish with Curried Sweetbreads

Monkfish is a large, meaty fish that lends itself to the slow braising used in this recipe. Its mild taste allows it to absorb the complex flavors of this unusual and intriguing curry sauce seasoned, in part, with fresh banana.

To Drink

Dry Riesling, Gewürztraminer
Fifth Floor recommends: 1995
Zind Humbrecht Clos St. Urbain
Riesling, Alsace

Curry Sauce

2 tablespoons grapeseed oil or olive oil
1 carrot, peeled and diced
1 small white onion, diced
2 stalks celery, minced
1 jalapeno chile, minced
4 cloves garlic, minced
1-inch piece young fresh ginger, peeled and minced
3 tablespoons garam masala
4 cups Fish Fumet (page 207), Chicken Stock (page 205), or water
1 ripe banana
$1/2$ cup coconut milk
Juice of 1 lime
Kosher salt and freshly ground pepper to taste

Sweetbreads

2 tablespoons kosher salt, plus more to taste
1 pound veal sweetbreads, soaked overnight in milk and drained
1 tablespoon grapeseed or olive oil
3 shallots, thinly sliced
Freshly ground pepper to taste
1 cup Madeira wine
Juice of 1 lime
2 tablespoons unsalted butter

Monkfish

Four 8-ounce fillets monkfish, bone-in

Kosher salt and freshly ground pepper to taste
2 tablespoons grapeseed oil or olive oil

To make the curry sauce, heat the grapeseed oil in a large, heavy saucepan over low heat. Add the carrot, onion, celery, jalapeno, garlic, and ginger and sauté, stirring occasionally, until the vegetables begin to soften, about 10 minutes. Do not let them brown. Add the garam masala and the fumet. Increase the heat to medium and bring to a boil. Reduce the heat to low and simmer until the vegetables are very soft. Peel and mash the banana and stir it into the mixture. Pour the mixture into a blender and process until smooth. Strain through a fine-meshed sieve, pressing on the solids with the back of a large spoon. Return to a clean saucepan and stir in the coconut milk and lime juice. Season with salt and pepper and set aside.

To prepare the sweetbreads, fill a large pot three-quarters full with water, add the 2 tablespoons salt, and bring to a boil over high heat. Blanch the sweetbreads for 2 minutes. Using a slotted spoon, transfer them to a bowl of ice water for 1 minute. Drain thoroughly, dry on a tea towel, and carefully remove the outer membrane. Cut the sweetbreads into 4 equal portions and set them aside.

Heat the grapeseed oil in a sauté pan over medium-low heat, add the shallots, and sauté until they begin to caramelize, about 30 minutes. Do not let them burn. Season the sweetbreads with salt and pepper, add them to the pan with the shallots, and turn off the heat. Add the Madeira and lime juice. Carefully turn the heat to medium-low so that the Madeira does not ignite. Braise the sweetbreads until all the liquid is evaporated and the sugars from the Madeira begin to caramelize. Transfer the sweetbreads to a plate and keep warm. Swirl the butter in the pan until it is just melted. Remove from the heat and keep warm.

Preheat the oven to 400°. Season the monkfish on both sides with salt and pepper. Heat the grapeseed oil in a large ovenproof sauté pan and sear the monkfish for 2 to 3 minutes on each side, or until golden brown. Transfer the pan to the oven and roast the fish until opaque throughout, about 8 minutes. Remove from the oven and let rest 5 minutes.

To serve, heat the curry sauce and the sweetbreads if necessary. Spoon several tablespoons of curry sauce onto each of 4 warm dinner plates. Place a monkfish fillet on each plate, top with a piece of sweetbread, and spoon some of the caramelized shallots on top. Serve immediately.

SERVES 4

FRINGALE

Gerald Hirigoyen
Executive Chef

"...When I walk into San Sebastian's fish market and see the glistening displays, I want to buy everything at once," Gerald Hirigoyen writes in his book *The Basque Kitchen.* "Langoustine, sole, hake, squid, fresh tuna, spider crab, salmon, sardines, and anchovies snuggle in seaweed beds arranged on slanting marble counters," he continues; "...No wonder Basque chefs have a reputation as the best seafood cooks in Europe."

Gerald Hirigoyen's homeland is the Basque country, that region of France and Spain nestled in the western slopes of the Pyrenees, where the Bay of Biscay slaps against the sandy beaches. Although his sister restaurants, Fringale and Pastis, are not exclusively Basque, the exuberant style of this cuisine is a signature element.

Fringale, which means "hunger pang," set the standard for a new generation of bistros. By day, it is packed with business customers; by night, the diminutive room takes on a golden glow, the pace slows, and Fringale becomes an inviting place to linger. In 1995, Gerald was voted Chef of the Year by *San Francisco Focus* magazine. Across town is Gerald's second restaurant, Pastis, also in a small space, like Fringale, but with an emphasis on the flavors of the Mediterranean. When the restaurant opened, a bottle of absinthe sat above the bar, a tribute to France's signature liqueur, which was replaced by pastis after absinthe was banned. So many customers wanted a taste that eventually the bottle was moved out of sight.

570 FOURTH STREET

(415) 543-0573

Tuna Steak with Potato, Chorizo, and Onion Ragout

This boldly flavored recipe features the aromatic peppers of the Basque village of Espelette. If you have some, use it; if not, use paprika. I like to add a pinch of chipotle powder to Hungarian paprika to mimic the mildly smoky quality of the *piment d'Espelette*. Be sure to use Spanish chorizo (which is flavored with Spanish paprika) and not Mexican chorizo, which is quite different from the coarse-textured dried sausage called for here.

4 1/2 tablespoons olive oil
1 onion, diced
5 large cloves garlic, crushed
3 ounces Spanish chorizo, thinly sliced
1 teaspoon minced fresh thyme
2 pounds russet potatoes, peeled and thickly sliced
1 cup dry white wine
5 threads of saffron
2 1/2 cups Chicken Stock (page 205)
1/4 teaspoon *piment d'Espelette* or paprika
1 tablespoon extra virgin olive oil
2 tablespoons minced fresh flat-leaf parsley
Four 6-ounce tuna steaks, each about 1 inch thick
Sea salt and freshly ground pepper to taste

Heat 3 tablespoons of the olive oil in a large, heavy saucepan or flameproof casserole over medium heat. Add the onion and garlic and sauté for about 3 minutes. Add the chorizo and thyme and sauté for 3 minutes more. Add the potatoes, wine, and saffron, bring to a boil, and cook until the liquid is reduced by half, 6 or 7 minutes. Add the chicken stock and return to a boil. Add the salt, cover, and reduce heat to medium. Simmer until the potatoes are tender, about 20 minutes. Remove from the heat and add the *piment d'Espelette*, the 1 tablespoon extra virgin olive oil, and the parsley. Swirl the pan several times to bind the ingredients. Set aside.

Heat the remaining 1 1/2 tablespoons of olive oil in a large sauté pan over high heat. Season the tuna on both sides with salt and pepper, and sear for 1 minute on each side, or until seared on the outside but rare inside. Spoon a bed of the ragout in the center of 4 plates, place a tuna steak on top, and serve immediately.

SERVES 4

John Dory with Braised Leeks, Wild Mushrooms, and Artichokes

Most John Dory in the United States is from New Zealand; it is not true John Dory, but a close relative. American John Dory is fished off the coast of Florida. The flesh is firm, white, and lean.

To Drink

Pinot Blanc

Fringale recommends: Rosé Rioja

8 tablespoons olive oil

3 cloves garlic, thinly sliced

3 leeks, including pale green parts, diced

1 cup Chicken Stock (page 205)

2 shallots, finely diced

4 ounces chanterelle mushrooms

4 ounces shiitake mushrooms, stemmed

4 ounces oyster mushrooms

4 cooked artichoke hearts, cut into $1/4$-inch-thick slices (see page 202)

1 cup Veal Stock (page 209), or more chicken stock

Giusto's sea salt, finely ground sel gris, or kosher salt to taste

Freshly ground pepper to taste

4 tablespoons unsalted butter

Four 6-ounce John Dory fillets

Combine 3 tablespoons of the olive oil, the garlic, leeks, and chicken stock in a large, shallow saucepan over high heat. Bring the ingredients to a boil, reduce heat, cover, and simmer for 10 minutes, or until almost no liquid remains in the pan; set aside.

Heat 2 tablespoons of the olive oil in a large sauté pan over high heat. Add the shallots and all of the mushrooms and sauté for 5 minutes, or until the mushrooms are soft and lightly browned. Transfer the ingredients to the saucepan with the leeks. Add the artichokes. Place the saucepan over medium-high heat, add the veal stock, and bring to a gentle boil. Season with salt and pepper, then swirl in the butter until evenly incorporated.

Heat the remaining 3 tablespoons olive oil in a large nonstick sauté pan over medium-high heat. Season the fillets on both sides with salt and pepper and sauté for 2 minutes on each side, or until just cooked through. Spoon some of the mushroom mixture in the center of each plate, set a fillet on top, and serve immediately.

SERVES 4

Salmon Wrapped in Serrano Ham
with Garlic and Bread Sauce

Serrano ham, or *jamón serrano*, is an intensely flavored dry-cured ham from Spain. It's not unlike Italian prosciutto, which you can use in its place if necessary. It must be sliced thinly enough that it will wrap easily around the salmon.

5 tablespoons olive oil

$1/2$ small onion, thinly sliced

6 cloves garlic, crushed

$1/2$ cup dry white wine

1 cup Vegetable Stock (page 203)

Three or four $3/8$-inch-thick slices day-old baguette

Sea salt to taste

8 thin slices serrano ham

Four 6-ounce salmon fillets, each about 1 inch thick,
    pin bones removed (see page 100)

$1/2$ teaspoon extra virgin olive oil

Freshly ground black pepper to taste

To Drink

Chardonnay, dry Rosé, Beaujolais

Fringale recommends: Dry white wine from Irouléguy, in the French Basque country

Braised Greens

$1/3$ cup water

3 tablespoons unsalted butter

2 pounds braising greens

Sea salt and freshly ground black pepper to taste

Garnish

1 tablespoon minced fresh flat-leaf parsley

8 large diagonally sliced croutons (optional)

Preheat the oven to 425°. To make the bread sauce, heat 2 tablespoons of the olive oil in a saucepan over medium heat. Add the onion and garlic and sauté until golden brown and lightly caramelized, about 5 minutes. Add the wine, vegetable stock, bread, and salt and bring to a boil. Decrease the heat slightly and simmer for 20 minutes. Transfer the ingredients to a blender and blend on high speed until liquefied; set aside in the blender until just before serving.

To prepare the fillets, evenly arrange 2 slices of the ham lengthwise on a work surface so that they slightly overlap. Place a salmon fillet centered horizontally at the bottom of the ham slices and carefully roll the fillet up in the ham. Set it aside, seam-side down. Repeat with the remaining 6 slices of ham and 3 fillets.

Heat the remaining 3 tablespoons olive oil in a large ovenproof nonstick sauté pan over high heat. Place the wrapped fillets in the pan, seam-side down. Transfer the pan to the oven and roast the fillets for 5 minutes. Turn the fillets over and continue to roast for 4 to 5 minutes, or until slightly opaque in the center.

Meanwhile, add the $1/2$ teaspoon extra virgin olive oil and the pepper to the bread sauce. Blend again quickly, just long enough to incorporate the oil. Strain the sauce through a fine-meshed sieve into a small saucepan. Place over low heat to warm slightly.

To prepare the braising greens, combine the water, butter, braising greens, and salt and pepper in a large saucepan. Cover and cook over high heat just until greens wilt, about 5 minutes.

To serve, place a small bed of greens in the center of each plate. Lay 1 salmon fillet on top of the greens and spoon the sauce on top of and around the edges of the dish. Sprinkle with parsley and set 2 croutons at 2 o'clock on each plate. Serve immediately.

SERVES 4

GARY DANKO

Gary Danko
Chef and Co-owner

G<small>ARY</small> D<small>ANKO</small> is widely acknowledged as one of the most talented American chefs of his generation. A protégé of Madeleine Kamman, the renowned chef, teacher, and cookbook author, Gary was named Best California Chef in the 1995 James Beard Awards. Both the Dining Room at the Ritz-Carlton and Viognier at Draeger's in San Mateo were named Best New Restaurant by *Esquire* magazine during Gary's tenure. Within months of the opening of Gary Danko, *Esquire* honored Danko's efforts a third time, naming the new eatery Best New Restaurant in the December 1999 issue. In the spring and summer of 2000, similar accolades followed from the James Beard Foundation and *San Francisco* magazine. Danko is known for a distinctive style that is at once sophisticated yet casual, exuberant yet refined.

800 N<small>ORTH</small> P<small>OINT</small>

(415) 399-0499

Salmon Ceviche with Green Chiles and Lime

To Drink

Bock beer, red ale

Gary Danko recommends:

margaritas, limeade

Before you dice the salmon, remove the pin bones—those delicate little bones that run perpendicular to the skin. Run the tips of your fingers over the surface of the fillet to locate the bones. Use one hand to hold the fish in place and the other to grab onto each bone with a pair of needle-nose pliers and pull gently until the bone comes free. (Keep the pliers with other kitchen utensils and use only with food.)

1 pound salmon fillet, cut into $1/4$-inch dice

$1/3$ cup freshly squeezed lime juice

2 fresh green Anaheim chiles

3 tablespoons extra virgin olive oil

3 tomatoes, peeled, seeded, and diced (see page 218)

1 tablespoon minced fresh flat-leaf parsley

$1/2$ cup cilantro sprigs, minced

$1/2$ serrano chile, minced

2 teaspoons kosher salt

$1 1/2$ teaspoons cumin seed, toasted and ground (see page 216)

$1/2$ teaspoon minced garlic (about 1 small clove)

2 tablespoons finely julienned mint leaves

4 drops Tabasco sauce

2 avocados, cut in half, pitted, and peeled

Combine the salmon and lime juice in a glass bowl and let sit, covered, at room temperature for 1 hour. Meanwhile, roast the Anaheim chiles over a gas flame until they are evenly blackened, about 5 minutes. Let cool, peel, and discard the skin and seeds. Cut the chiles into $1/4$-inch dice.

Drain all of the liquid off the salmon and discard it. Add the olive oil, tomatoes, roasted chiles, parsley, cilantro, serrano chile, salt, cumin, garlic, mint, and Tabasco sauce. Taste and correct the seasoning. To serve, cut the avocado into lengthwise slices, fan several slices on individual plates, and divide the ceviche among the servings. Serve immediately.

SERVES 6

Oyster Bisque with Armagnac

Bottled clam juice is available in most supermarkets. It has a fairly intense flavor; if any of your guests have a timid palate, you can replace the clam juice with an equal amount of fish fumet for a more subtle soup.

9 tablespoons unsalted butter

$1/_3$ cup minced onion

$1/_3$ cup minced celery

$1/_3$ cup minced carrot

1 bay leaf

$1/_2$ teaspoon dried thyme

$1/_3$ cup dry white wine

4 cups Fish Fumet (page 207)

2 cups clam juice

1 pint shucked oysters, such as Hog Island Sweetwaters or Kumamoto
    (liquor reserved)

2 cups heavy whipping cream

Kosher salt and freshly ground pepper to taste

2 to 3 tablespoons Armagnac or brandy

2 tablespoons snipped fresh chives for garnish

Melt the butter in a heavy soup pot over medium heat. Stir in the onion, celery, carrot, bay leaf, and thyme and sauté, stirring occasionally, until the onion is translucent, about 10 minutes. Add the wine, fish fumet, clam juice, and oyster liquor. Bring to a boil, reduce the heat to low, and simmer until the liquid is reduced by half, about 10 minutes. Stir in the cream, return to a boil, and season with salt and pepper. Strain the liquid through a fine-meshed sieve, pressing hard on the vegetables with the back of a large spoon to extract as much liquid as possible. Return the soup to low heat, add the Armagnac and the oysters, and poach briefly until the oysters just barely firm up, about 30 seconds. Ladle into warm soup plates, sprinkle with chives, and serve immediately.

SERVES 4 TO 6

Sautéed Trout with Pancetta and Asparagus

For the very best trout, you have to either catch it yourself or find a market that keeps live trout in tanks. If you can't get live trout, the pancetta, garlic, and parsley in this recipe will give blander commercial trout a good boost in flavor.

To Drink

Sauvignon Blanc

Gary Danko recommends: Nigl Grüner Veltliner, Alte Reben (Old Vines), Kremstal, Austria 1998

6 asparagus spears, cut into 2-inch lengths
2 ounces pancetta, cut into $1/_4$-inch dice
2 trout, 8 to 10 ounces each, boned, trimmed, and separated into fillets
Kosher salt and freshly ground pepper to taste
$1/_2$ cup all-purpose flour, seasoned with salt and pepper
2 tablespoons olive oil or vegetable oil
2 tablespoons Clarified Butter (page 201)
2 to 3 cloves garlic, minced
2 tablespoons minced fresh flat-leaf parsley

Blanch the asparagus in a large pot of salted boiling water for 30 seconds. Drain thoroughly, plunge into ice water, and drain thoroughly again. Set the asparagus aside.

Sauté the pancetta in a 10-inch nonstick sauté pan over medium-low heat until it is cooked through but not crisp. Transfer the pancetta and any rendered fat (there will not be much) to a small bowl.

Season the trout fillets with salt and pepper, dredge them in flour, and shake them to remove excess flour. Heat the olive oil in the same sauté pan over medium heat and place the trout fillets, skin-side down, in the pan. Agitate the pan gently and cook until the fish begin to turn opaque around the edges and the skin is crisp. Turn, cook for 1 minute, and transfer to individual plates. Use a paper towel to wipe the sauté pan clean. Return the pan to medium heat and add the butter. When the butter is melted, add the asparagus and pancetta. Cook until heated through, 4 to 5 minutes. Remove from the heat, stir in the garlic and parsley and season with salt and pepper to taste. Pour the mixture over the trout and serve immediately.

SERVES 4

GREAT EASTERN

Chi Sun Lai
Owner

Beyond the entryway of Great Eastern, a backlit green and white sign lists the day's seafood: spot prawns, Dungeness crab, grass rockfish, China cod, scallops, clams, oysters, abalone, geoduck, sculpin, frogs, and a myriad of other mysterious creatures. This seafood is alive, kept in tanks that flank the wall at the back of the dining room. If you order from the extensive written menu, you'll have a good meal. Make your selection from the list of live fish and let your server suggest the preparation, and your meal may be sensational. For fresher fish, you'll have to catch it yourself and cook it on the spot.

Owner Chi Sun Lai employs cooks, not an executive chef. With thirty years' experience, he runs his own ship and handpicks all of the fish himself, from Chinese distributors who come to his door. It's not uncommon to see vendors walking through the dining room holding a tub of flopping fish, water splashing everywhere. Look towards the back wall to watch the fish be plunged into the tanks to await their fate. After a small fish is killed, its head and bones are simmered in a strong stock with straw mushrooms, bean cake, and mustard greens for soup. The fillet is cut up and stir-fried over very high heat. Large fish are served three ways: The bones and head are made into soup, the midsection is steamed, and the muscular tail is braised. Stocks and sauces go through a lengthy cooking time of ten hours, twenty hours, and more—but the seafood comes to you within minutes of its final living moments.

649 JACKSON STREET

(415) 986-2500

Minced Seafood in Lettuce Leaves

In 1999, I had the opportunity to visit Akiak, a small fishing village on Alitak Bay on Kodiak Island, Alaska, established by Russians in the early 1800s. Today several dozen fish camps ring the nearby inland bays, and the region is becoming known for its superior sockeye salmon with a deep scarlet flesh and rich flavor. I spent several days at the camp operated by the Barker family on Olga Bay, where we picked salmon from gillnets and used a line to catch halibut and Dolly Vardon trout. One day we loaded long-handled nets into the skiff and went in search of sea cucumbers. The unusual-looking creatures—deep reddish brown and cucumber shaped—covered the floor of the shallows not far from camp; we had a bucketful in about fifteen minutes. Back on shore, we cleaned them by hooking them on nails hammered into a big board, cutting them in half lengthwise, and then using a sharp knife to peel off the thin fillet of meat that lines the inside of the thick, tough skin. It wasn't difficult, but it took practice to get the hang of it. If you can get fresh sea cucumbers for this dish, great. If not, use squid; sea cucumbers taste similar, though their flavor is a little stronger and their texture a little softer.

To Drink

Lager, pilsner

Great Eastern recommends:

Tsingtao beer

1 tablespoon kosher salt, plus more for seasoning

8 ounces frozen octopus, thawed, blanched for 2 minutes, and drained

1 to 2 tablespoons vegetable oil

6 very fresh jumbo shrimp, shelled and deveined (see page 219)

4 fresh sea scallops, shucked

1 to 2 sea cucumbers, cleaned, or 2 small calamari bodies, cleaned and peeled (see page 219)

2 cloves garlic, minced

$1/2$ teaspoon grated fresh ginger

Red pepper flakes

Asian sesame oil

Freshly ground pepper to taste

Lettuce leaves, preferably from iceberg lettuce

Fill a medium pot half full with water, add the 1 tablespoon kosher salt, and bring to a boil over high heat. Reduce the heat to medium, add the octopus, and simmer until it is tender when pierced with a fork, about 1 hour. Cool the octopus in ice water, drain it, and dry it.

While the octopus is cooking, heat 1 tablespoon of the oil in a wok or sauté pan over high heat, add the shrimp, and cook until they just turn pink, 2 to 3 minutes. Transfer to a plate. Return the pan to high heat, add the scallops, cook for 2 minutes, turn, and cook for 2 minutes more, or until golden brown. Add the scallops to the plate of shrimp. Return the pan to high heat again, add another tablespoon of oil if the pan seems dry, and cook the sea cucumbers or squid until it turns opaque, about 1 minute.

When the seafood is cool enough to handle, cut it into small dice and put it in a medium bowl. Add the garlic, ginger, red pepper flakes, and several shakes of sesame oil and toss gently. Season with salt and pepper and toss again. Cover the bowl and refrigerate until chilled, about 2 hours.

To serve, put the seafood in a mound in the center of a serving plate and surround it with lettuce leaves. Guests take a leaf, put a little of the seafood mixture in it, fold the leaf over, and eat.

SERVES 4 TO 6

Chilled Dungeness Crab with Chinese Wine

As Chi Sun Lai describes the succulent goodness of his marinated Dungeness crab, I have to stop myself from licking my fingers, his description is that vivid. The secrets to this recipe are to begin with live crabs, don't cook them too long, and make sure your stock is a robust one.

To Drink

Red ale

Great Eastern recommends:

Tsingtao beer

6 cups Strong Stock (page 206)

3 cups Shaoxing wine or dry sherry

$1/4$ cup grated fresh ginger

4 to 5 cloves garlic, crushed

1 bunch green onions, including green parts, sliced

2 live Dungeness crabs, cooked and cleaned (see page 220) but left whole (bodies and legs still connected)

Bring the stock and wine to a boil in a medium soup pot. Stir in the ginger, garlic, and green onions. Remove from the heat, add the crab, and let cool to room temperature. Cover and refrigerate the crab in the liquid for 24 hours. Remove the crab from the liquid. Using a cleaver or large knife, cut the bodies in half. Twist off the legs and serve immediately.

SERVES 3 TO 4

Jook with Salmon

Jook, also called congee and rice porridge, is served throughout Asia, from Korea to Borneo and Sumatra. It is said to be a guarantee against hangover; it is also just plain good. Great Eastern offers a half-dozen versions, but if you order it too early in the day, it won't be ready. Because they're open late, though, Great Eastern's jook can be a wonderful restorative after a night on the town. At home, you can make this jook without the salmon and use any leftover shellfish, fish, roasted chicken, or shredded pork on top.

$^2/_3$ cup short-grain rice

1 tablespoon peanut oil

Kosher salt to taste

3 cups Light Chicken Broth (page 204)
    or Chicken Stock (page 205)

4 cups water

Grilled Salmon (recipe follows)

2 or 3 tablespoons Asian sesame oil

1 tablespoon soy sauce, plus more to taste

1 teaspoon grated fresh ginger

Red pepper flakes to taste

2 tablespoons minced fresh cilantro for garnish

3 green onions, including some green parts,
    cut into very thin rounds, for garnish

Rinse the rice in several changes of cold water until the water is no longer cloudy. Drain. Heat the 1 tablespoon peanut oil in a large saucepan over high heat. Add the rice, stir, and season with salt. Add the chicken broth and water. Bring to a boil and cook for 4 minutes. Decrease the heat to low and simmer, covered, for $1^1/_2$ to 2 hours, stirring occasionally, until the rice has the texture and consistency of soft porridge. The mixture should be creamy and fairly homogeneous.

Ladle the rice into 4 large soup bowls. Break the salmon into chunks and divide it among the portions. In a small bowl, mix together the sesame oil, soy sauce, ginger, and red pepper flakes. Spoon some of the sauce over the salmon and rice. Garnish with the cilantro and green onions. Serve immediately with additional soy sauce for seasoning.

SERVES 4

Grilled Salmon

1 pound salmon fillets, pin bones removed (see page 100)
2 teaspoons sesame oil
Kosher salt and freshly ground pepper to taste
$1/_3$ cup soy sauce
2 tablespoons dry sherry
2 tablespoons brown sugar

Heat a stovetop grill pan over medium heat. Brush the salmon on both sides with the sesame oil and season with salt and pepper. Heat the soy sauce, sherry, and sugar in a small saucepan over low heat, stirring continuously until the sugar is dissolved. Cook the salmon, skin-side up, for 5 minutes. Turn the salmon over, brush it generously with sauce, and cook until the skin is crispy and the salmon is cooked through but still translucent in the center, 4 to 5 minutes. Brush with more sauce and remove from the heat.

LULU

Jody Denton
Executive Chef

THE APPEAL OF FIRE is an atavistic attraction, I think, a fascination that we carry with us in our very cells. When the fire blazes upward towards the high ceiling of LuLu, we experience a visceral thrill, a pleasure that becomes palpable when we taste the foods, such as smoky pan-roasted mussels, that have been licked by these flames. Mmmm—when those mussels are in your mouth, it's almost impossible to remember anything that ever tasted better.

Today, Jody Denton presides over the cavernous eatery that was once the proving ground of Reed Hearon, Rose Pistola's well-known owner. When Hearon moved on, Jody took the helm. Under his guidance, LuLu's cuisine evolved slowly and thoughtfully, as Jody kept many signature dishes on the menu and sought inspiration for new ones from the entire Mediterranean region. Today, in spite of a daunting noise level, LuLu is a delightful destination with an alluring menu and an excellent selection of oysters on the half shell.

In 1999, Jody Denton opened Azie, a hip, stylish eatery where he indulges his preference for inventive East-West cuisine. At Azie, which is next door to LuLu, seafood dishes like crab pôt de crème, sardine tempura, and steamed fish fillets slathered with melted foie gras are shaped by both European and Asian techniques and ingredients.

816 FOLSOM STREET

(415) 495-5775

Olive Oil–Poached Tuna Niçoise

Not so long ago, salade niçoise, a classic dish from the south of France, was served with canned tuna, still the most traditional way to make it. In the 1980s, versions made with fresh tuna and even fresh-roasted chicken began to appear on restaurant menus and in cookbooks. Although I've heard several French cooks complain about this adaptation, any version of the salad will be great if it is made with good ingredients. Here, chef Jody Denton poaches the tuna in olive oil, a technique that gives the fish an even richer flavor than it already has. (Fresh fava beans have a very short season in early spring; at other times, simply omit them.) the anchoiade really makes this salad special, so I urge you to use it if you feel comfortable doing so. See page xv for my thoughts on egg safety.

To Drink

Dry Rosé, Marsanne
LuLu recommends: 1998 Walter Hansel Chardonnay Russian River Valley

3 eggs, room temperature

8 ounces fingerling potatoes

1 tablespoon kosher salt, plus more for seasoning

Freshly ground pepper to taste

4 cups extra virgin olive oil (see note, opposite)

1 1/2 pounds yellowfin tuna fillet, trimmed and cut into 4 to 6 pieces (1 per serving)

4 ounces Blue Lake green beans, blanched for 3 to 4 minutes and chilled

1 pound fresh fava beans, shelled, blanched for 1 minute, and peeled

4 ounces cherry tomatoes

1 small sweet onion (such as Walla Walla), very thinly sliced

1 red or yellow bell pepper, seeded, deribbed, and cut into thin rounds

1 bunch small red radishes, thinly sliced

2 cups young salad greens, such as mâche, arugula, or mixed greens

2 tablespoons best-quality extra virgin olive oil

Anchoiade (recipe follows)

Put the eggs in a small pan and add water to cover by 1 inch. Bring to a boil over medium heat, reduce the heat to low, and cook for 4 minutes. Remove from the heat and let rest in the hot water for 4 minutes. Drain the eggs. Put the potatoes in a medium pan and add water to cover by 1 inch. Add 1 tablespoon kosher salt, bring to a boil over medium heat, reduce the heat to medium-low, and cook until the potatoes are tender when pierced with a fork, 15 to 20 minutes. Drain, cool, and cut in half lengthwise. Season with salt and pepper and set aside.

Meanwhile, heat the 4 cups of olive oil in a deep pan over medium-low heat to 190°. Season each piece of tuna on both sides with salt and pepper, submerge all the fish in the oil at once and cook for 5 minutes. Using a wire mesh strainer, transfer the fish to a warm platter.

Peel the eggs. Place a piece of tuna in the center of 4 to 6 individual serving plates and arrange the vegetables and greens around the tuna. Cut the eggs in half lengthwise (the yolks will be soft), and add one to each serving. Drizzle the vegetables and greens with the best-quality olive oil, season with salt and pepper, top the tuna with a spoonful of anchoiade, and serve immediately.

SERVES 4 TO 6

Note: Use extra virgin olive oil to cook the tuna, but not an expensive one. The flavor of olive oil deteriorates at temperatures above 140°.

Anchoiade

....

1 egg yolk
6 salt-cured anchovies, rinsed and dried
2 teaspoons Dijon mustard
1 tablespoon freshly squeezed lemon juice
1 cup extra virgin olive oil
1 tablespoon minced fresh flat-leaf parsley
Kosher salt and freshly ground black pepper to taste

Put the egg yolk, anchovies, mustard, and lemon juice in a food processor and pulse until smooth. With the machine running, gradually add the olive oil. Transfer to a small bowl, stir in the parsley, and season with salt and pepper to taste. Cover and refrigerate for up to 5 days.

MAKES ABOUT 1 CUP

Bourride of Halibut

Bourride is one of two traditional fish soups from Provence—bouillabaisse is the other. Bourride most often refers to a soup thickened with a liaison such as aioli, egg yolks, or both. Bouillabaisse is usually served with rouille or aioli alongside.

To Drink

Champagne, dry Rosé
LuLu recommends: Pommery Brut
Rosé, NV, Champagne

1 baguette, thinly sliced
2 pounds halibut steaks
Kosher salt and freshly ground pepper to taste
1 tablespoon olive oil
8 cloves garlic, slivered
1 small leek (white part only), cut in to thin rounds
1 small carrot, peeled and cut into $1/4$-inch dice
1 small zucchini, cut into $1/4$-inch dice
1 small yellow squash, cut into $1/4$-inch dice
12 ounces small new potatoes, quartered
8 cups Fish Fumet (page 207) or Light Chicken Broth (page 204)
1 cup Aioli (page 211)
1 tablespoon minced fresh flat-leaf parsley
1 tablespoon snipped fresh chives
1 tablespoon minced fresh chervil

Preheat the oven to 250°. Place the baguette slices on baking sheets in a single layer and toast, turning once, in the oven until they are crisp and golden brown on both sides, 15 to 20 minutes. Let cool and set aside.

Season the halibut steaks on both sides with salt and pepper. Heat the olive oil in a large skillet over medium-high heat until very hot. Add the halibut and sear for 2 minutes. Decrease the heat to medium-low, turn the fish, and add the garlic, leek, carrot, zucchini, squash, and potatoes. Stir and toss the vegetables for 2 minutes. Add the fumet and bring to a boil. Decrease the heat to a simmer and cook for 5 minutes.

Use a slotted metal spatula to transfer the fish to individual shallow bowls. Stir 2 tablespoons of the hot broth into the aioli, then add 2 more tablespoons of hot broth and mix thoroughly. Add the parsley, chives, and chervil to the hot broth mixture. Stir in the tempered aioli and heat through for 1 minute; do not boil. Ladle the hot broth and vegetables over the fish. Serve immediately, with the toasted baguette alongside.

SERVES 4 TO 6

Seared Calamari with Creamy Polenta

In northern Italy, where polenta has been a staple for centuries, seafood is traditionally served with white polenta, which is made from white rather than yellow corn. If you have white polenta, use it here for a very traditional dish; keep in mind, though, that it has a slightly gelatinous texture that some people find objectionable. I think it is both delicious and visually appealing, a beautiful canvas for the delicate squid. Moretti, an Italian brand that is fairly easy to find in the United States, produces an excellent white polenta.

Parsley Butter

$1/_2$ cup (1 stick) unsalted butter at room temperature
2 tablespoons minced fresh flat-leaf parsley
2 tablespoons minced garlic
1 tablespoon grated lemon zest
Kosher salt and freshly ground pepper to taste

Four 1-inch-thick slices sourdough bread, crusts removed
2 tablespoons extra virgin olive oil
1 pound small cleaned calamari, tentacles separated,
    bodies cut into $1/_2$-inch-wide rings (see page 219)
Kosher salt and freshly ground pepper to taste
$1 1/_2$ tablespoons olive oil
Creamy Polenta (page 213)
1 lemon, cut into wedges, for garnish

To Drink

Soave Classico
LuLu recommends: 1998 Soave
Classico Superior, 'La Rocca',
Pieropan

Combine the butter, parsley, garlic, and lemon zest in a blender or food processor. Season with salt and pepper and pulse to mix ingredients thoroughly. Taste and correct the seasoning. Transfer to a bowl, cover, refrigerate for up to 1 day.

Preheat the oven to 275°. Tear the bread into pieces, spread them out on a baking sheet, and toast in the oven until almost completely dry but not browned, about 12 minutes. Let cool to room temperature. Pulse the toasted bread in a blender or food processor to make evenly coarse crumbs; do not make the crumbs too fine. Toss the bread crumbs with the extra virgin olive oil and season with salt and pepper. Spread the crumbs out on a baking sheet and toast in the oven until golden brown. Set aside.

Put the calamari in a bowl and season with salt and pepper. Heat the mild olive oil in a large, heavy sauté pan over high heat. Add the calamari, spreading it evenly over the bottom of the pan. Do not stir for 30 seconds, then toss. Cook undisturbed for 30 seconds more, or until the calamari releases its liquid. Continue to cook until the liquid evaporates, about 30 seconds. Add 2 tablespoons of the parsley butter and continue cooking over high heat until the butter turns golden brown and fragrant, about 3 minutes. Remove from the heat and toss with a generous handful of bread crumbs. Melt the remaining butter in a small saucepan.

To serve, divide the polenta among individual bowls. Top with the calamari, drizzle with the remaining butter, and scatter with the remaining bread crumbs. Garnish with lemon wedges and serve immediately.

SERVES 4 TO 6

San Francisco Bay Ferries

When the Loma Prieta earthquake of October 17, 1989, closed the Bay Bridge for several weeks, commuters from the East Bay were forced onto ferries, some for the first time. Unfortunately, the alternative route to San Francisco did not catch on and ferry service from this part of the Bay Area has been mostly discontinued. In Marin County, commuters head to San Francisco from Larkspur, Tiburon, and Sausalito, and others commute across the Bay from as far away as Vallejo. Visitors in San Francisco can catch ferries from Fisherman's Wharf and from the Ferry Building at the foot of Market Street; some offer tours of the Bay, and some offer transportation across it.

MC^2

Yoshi Kojima
Executive Chef

IN AN OLD WAREHOUSE from the historic Barbary Coast era, architect Mark Cavagnero has designed one of the most dramatic restaurant interiors in the city, a montage of brick, wood, chrome, fabric, and filtered sunlight, a highly successful recipe for seductive atmosphere. Chef Yoshi Kojima may be as inspired by his restaurant's interior as his customers are. His food is signature 1990s architectural fare, dramatically presented dishes that must be deconstructed before they are eaten. Several seafood dishes shine at mc^2, such as tuna tartare, seared tuna, and luscious pan-roasted salmon in a sea of Pinot Noir sauce. When you don't have time for a meal here, you can always stop by in the late afternoon for a drink at the bar, where an outstanding selection of wines are available by the glass.

470 PACIFIC AVENUE
(415) 956-0666

Fresh Sardines with Red Onion
and Baby Arugula Salad

Usually, sardines travel the California coast from south to north. Although fresh sardines are always good, the best time to catch them is between the summer and the fall when their flavor is at its peak. That's why local bluefin tuna also travel the same route every year: The tuna know good fish.

To Drink

India pale ale

mc² recommends: Geuze Boon
lambic ale, Belgium

16 fresh local sardines (about 18 ounces), pan-dressed and filleted
1 tablespoon minced fresh flat-leaf parsley
1 teaspoon minced fresh thyme
2 cloves garlic, crushed
9 1/2 teaspoons extra virgin olive oil
1 tablespoon freshly squeezed lemon juice
Kosher salt and freshly ground pepper to taste
1 cup thinly sliced red onion
1 tablespoon red wine vinegar
2 cups baby arugula
Bread Crumb Topping (recipe follows)

Put the sardines in a baking dish. Combine the parsley, thyme, garlic, and 5 tablespoons of the olive oil in a small bowl. Spoon the marinade over the sardines, cover, and refrigerate overnight.

To make the vinaigrette, put the lemon juice in a small bowl, season with salt and pepper, and gradually whisk in 2 1/2 tablespoons of the olive oil. Set aside.

Soak the red onion in cool water for 5 minutes. Drain thoroughly and dry on a tea towel. Put the onion in a small bowl and sprinkle with the red wine vinegar. Set aside for 5 minutes.

To serve, remove the sardines from the marinade. Heat the remaining 2 tablespoons olive oil in a sauté pan over medium-high heat and cook the sardines, skin-side down, until just cook through and slightly firm, 3 to 4 minutes.

Meanwhile, put the arugula and onions in a bowl, toss with the lemon vinaigrette, and divide among 4 serving plates. Drape the cooked sardines over the salad, then spoon some of the bread crumb mixture on top and around the edges. Serve immediately.

SERVES 4

Bread Crumb Topping

1 tablespoon golden raisins

1 tablespoon black raisins

3 tablespoons dry marsala wine

2 tablespoons extra virgin olive oil

1 bay leaf

3 anchovy fillets, rinsed

2 tablespoons pine nuts

1 cup fresh bread crumbs (see page 217)

Combine the raisins in a small bowl. Pour the marsala over them and set aside for 30 minutes. Drain.

Heat the olive oil with the bay leaf in a large sauté pan over low heat until the leaf is fragrant. Add the anchovies and sauté, tossing occasionally, for 1 minute. Add the raisins and sauté until plumped, about 2 minutes, then add the pine nuts and toss. Add the bread crumbs, stir, and sauté, tossing occasionally, until golden brown; do not let them burn. Let cool to room temperature.

MAKES ABOUT 1¹/₄ CUPS

Carpaccio of Bluefin Tuna
with Shiitake and Haricot Vert Salad

Bluefin tuna caught in Boston begin their journey in Florida. They travel north in search of food, often moving at speeds up to sixty miles per hour. By the time they reach Boston, they can weigh up to eight hundred pounds. These fish are highly prized in Japan because their bodies contain a substantial amount of fatty underbelly, or *toro*, a delicacy in sushi bars and Japanese restaurants. For a fascinating account of the traditional bluefin tuna harvest off the coast of Sicily, take a look at *Mattanza* by Therese Maggio.

To Drink

Dry Riesling, Sauvignon Blanc
mc^2 recommends: 1998 Leeuwin Estate Riesling, Margaret River, Australia

Four $1/8$-inch-thick slices fresh ginger
2 cloves garlic, sliced
$1\frac{1}{2}$ tablespoons soy sauce
2 tablespoons olive oil
12 small shiitake mushrooms, stemmed
12 ounces Boston bluefin tuna fillet, very thinly sliced
1 cup (about 3 ounces) haricots verts, blanched for 3 minutes, plunged into ice water, and drained
Kosher salt and freshly ground pepper to taste

Green Peppercorn Vinaigrette (recipe follows)

Combine the ginger, garlic, and soy sauce in a small bowl and set aside. Heat the olive oil in a small sauté pan over medium heat and sauté the shiitake caps until limp and tender, 7 to 8 minutes. Season with salt and pepper and toss with the ginger mixture. Set aside for 30 minutes.

To serve, arrange several slices of tuna on each of 4 individual plates. Toss the shiitakes and haricots together, season with salt and pepper, and place a small mound on top of the tuna. Drizzle the peppercorn vinaigrette over and around the tuna and serve immediately.

SERVES 4

Green Peppercorn Vinaigrette

4 teaspoons green peppercorns, drained and crushed

1 tablespoon minced shallot

1 teaspoon freshly squeezed lemon juice

1 teaspoon soy sauce

1 teaspoon minced fresh flat-leaf parsley

1 teaspoon snipped fresh chives

1 tablespoon extra virgin olive oil

Kosher salt and freshly ground pepper to taste

In a small bowl, combine the green peppercorns, shallot, lemon juice, soy sauce, parsley, and chives. Gradually whisk in the olive oil and season with salt and pepper.

MAKES ABOUT $^1/_4$ CUP

Grilled Pancetta-Wrapped Scallops with Caramelized Apple and Grilled Cèpes

Although scallops are available all year, their flavor begins to peak around December, coinciding with the peak of cèpe season. The delicate flavor and aroma of cèpes go beautifully with scallops, while pancetta ties them together. Be sure to check the mushrooms for worms, which often burrow inside the tasty fungi. If you find any, just discard the worms and continue with the recipe. Sierra Beauty apples are tart and not too sweet, and hold their structure well when cooked. If you can't find one, ask a grower or produce manager for a good substitute.

To Drink

Chardonnay

mc^2 recommends: 1997 Hubert Lamy Saint-Aubin en Remilly Premier Cru

12 sea scallops

12 thin slices pancetta

1 tablespoon sugar

1 Sierra Beauty apple, cored, peeled, and cut into thin slices

1 teaspoon unsalted butter

2 large fresh cèpe or porcini mushrooms, cut into
   8 lengthwise slices

Kosher salt and freshly ground pepper to taste

Extra virgin olive oil, as needed

Wrap each scallop in a slice of pancetta and secure it with a toothpick. Sprinkle the sugar in a medium sauté pan and cook over medium heat until the sugar dissolves and turns golden brown. Add the apple and turn the slices in the caramelized sugar to coat them thoroughly. Rub a plate with the butter and transfer the apple slices to the plate. Set aside and keep warm.

Prepare a hot fire in a charcoal grill or heat a stovetop grill pan. Season the porcini slices on both sides with salt and pepper and brush them lightly with olive oil. If using a charcoal grill, put the scallops and mushroom slices in an oiled grill basket. If using a grill pan, grill the scallops and mushrooms in batches, if necessary. Cook the scallops and mushrooms for 3 to 4 minutes on each side, or until golden brown.

To serve, arrange apple slices in the center of each of 4 plates, place 3 scallops on top, and arrange the mushroom slices around the scallops. Serve immediately.

SERVES 4

MASA'S

Chad Callahan
Executive Chef

THERE MAY BE NO FINER tribute to founding chef Masataka Kobayashi, whose 1985 murder has never been solved, than the fact that this remarkable restaurant still bears his name and enjoys the reputation for refined dining that he originally established. San Franciscans first became aware of Masa when he opened Auberge du Soleil in Rutherford, north of the city in Napa County; reviews of Auberge were simply breathtaking. When he launched Masa's, it was an immediate, overwhelming success; you had to make reservations months in advance. So popular was Masa's that customers took to selling their reservations to the highest bidder, a piece of San Francisco restaurant lore chronicled in Herb Caen's column. Masa's tragic death came at the height of his popularity.

Chad Callahan, who worked under chef Julian Serrano's direction in the early 1990s and became executive chef in 1997, has a style that is at once simple and sophisticated, elegant yet accessible. As luxurious as a meal at Masa's is, the food is neither fussy nor overly complicated; superior ingredients are allowed to speak for themselves. Chad looks to Bay Area fishermen, farmers, and cheese makers for his raw materials.

648 BUSH STREET
(415) 989-7154

Smoked Salmon and Cucumber Gougère

To Drink

Champagne, dry Rosé

Masa's recommends: Domaine
Tempier 1999 Bandol Rose

Here, chef Chad Callahan offers a simple appetizer that pairs the refreshing crispness of cucumber with the rich, deep flavors of smoked salmon. Served with a Blanc de Noir sparkling wine, these morsels offer a perfectly elegant and delicious beginning to a formal dinner. Because they are easy to eat while standing, they are also ideal for a cocktail party.

2 ounces smoked salmon, cut into $1/2$-inch dice

1 small English (hothouse) cucumber, peeled, seeded, and diced (about 1 cup)

3 tablespoons crème fraîche or sour cream

1 tablespoon minced fresh chives

1 tablespoon freshly squeezed lemon juice

4 tablespoons unsalted butter

$1/2$ teaspoon kosher salt

$1/2$ tablespoon sugar

1 cup water

$3/4$ cup all-purpose flour

4 eggs at room temperature

2 cups (8 ounces) shredded Gruyère cheese at room temperature

Toss the salmon, cucumber, crème fraîche, chives, and lemon juice together in a bowl. Cover and refrigerate.

In a medium saucepan, combine the butter, salt, sugar, and water. Cook over medium heat until the butter is melted. Add the flour and stir with a wooden spoon until the mixture pulls away from the sides of the pan. Stir in the eggs, one at a time, until well blended. Remove the pan from the heat and let cool to warm. Mix in the Gruyère until melted. Put the mixture in a large pastry bag fitted with a large round tip.

Line a baking sheet with parchment paper. Pipe the paste into rounds about the size of a quarter onto the prepared pan. Refrigerate until thoroughly chilled, about 1 hour.

Preheat the oven to 350°. Bake the pastries until golden brown, 30 to 35 minutes. Let cool slightly and cut in half crosswise. Spoon some of the salmon mixture into the bottom of each, replace the tops, and serve immediately.

SERVES 4 TO 6

Hog Island Oysters with Osetra Caviar and Beurre Vermouth

These voluptuously dressed oysters make a beautiful first course for a sit-down dinner. They do need last-minute attention, so it will be helpful if you have plates set up with the oyster shells in their nests of salt well before you begin. You can also reduce the wine earlier in the day and reheat it before you make the sauce.

2 cups dry white wine

1 cup dry white vermouth

1 bay leaf

1 shallot, minced

8 white peppercorns

1 tablespoon heavy whipping cream

$^{1}/_{2}$ cup (1 stick) cold unsalted butter, cut into tablespoon-sized
   pieces, plus 1 tablespoon

1 tablespoon freshly squeezed lemon juice

Kosher salt and freshly ground pepper to taste

16 oysters, preferably Hog Island Sweetwaters, shucked
   (shells and liquor reserved) (see page 221)

2 cups iodized salt

$^{1}/_{2}$ cup water

4 ounces osetra caviar

16 large spinach leaves

16 fresh chive tips for garnish

To Drink

Pinot Blanc, Sancerre

Masa's recommends: Charles
Schleret 1998 Pinot Blanc, Alsace

Pour the white wine into a saucepan and bring to a boil. Decrease the heat to a simmer and cook for 5 minutes. Remove from the heat and set aside. Combine the vermouth, bay leaf, shallot, and peppercorns in a small saucepan. Bring to a boil, decrease the heat to a simmer, and cook to reduce by two-thirds. Decrease the heat to low and add the cream. Add the $^{1}/_{2}$ cup of butter one piece at a time, whisking after each addition until the butter is melted. Add the lemon juice and season with salt and pepper. Strain through a fine-meshed sieve. Keep warm over tepid water.

Rinse and dry the oyster shells. In a large bowl, combine the salt and water. Place 4 dinner plates on a work surface. Using your hands, form balls of salt about the size of Ping-Pong balls and place 4 on each plate, leaving room between each one. Place an oyster shell on top of each salt ball, pressing down slightly.

Melting the remaining 1 tablespoon butter in a sauté pan over medium heat. Add the reserved oyster liquor and the spinach, and sauté them until limp, about 2 minutes. Drain off the excess liquid. Place a little of the wilted spinach in each oyster shell.

Bring the wine to a boil over medium heat, then decrease the heat to a simmer. In batches, poach the oysters in the wine for about 30 seconds, or until they just barely firm up. Using a small slotted spoon, transfer the oysters to the oyster shells. Spoon some of the hot beurre vermouth over each oyster, top with a small dollop of caviar, and garnish with a chive tip. Serve immediately.

SERVES 4

Heaven on the Half Shell

Raw oysters and clams expertly shucked (amateur shuckers often damage the delicate mollusks) and dressed with a squeeze of lemon, a dash of Tabasco, or a drizzle of tart mignonette are one of the world's great culinary pleasures. (Mignonette is a simple sauce of vinegar, lemon or lime juice, shallots, black pepper, and one or two other ingredients: minced ginger, perhaps, or jalapenos, cilantro, or tarragon). You certainly can prepare such a pristine feast at home, but the effortless indulgence of having it all set before you heightens the pleasure. Many San Francisco restaurants offer raw oysters and clams, but a few specialize in them, so you can stop by the bar for a quick fix instead of having them as a first course. Among the best locations to indulge in a little heaven on the half shell are Zuni Café, Belon, Swan Oyster Depot, PJ's Oyster Bed, the Elite Café, Anchor Oyster Bar, Yabbies Coastal Kitchen, and Absinthe.

Crispy Black Bass with Osetra Caviar Supreme Sauce

Here, chef Chad Callahan has created an extraordinarily appealing combination of flavors in a dish that is actually very simple to prepare. I use O olive oil; it is made by crushing organic Meyer lemons with ripe mission olives and it's absolutely delicious, not at all overpowering or artificial tasting as some lemon-flavored oils are. Chad uses Sciabica, a company that has been making olive oils in California for decades and that sells their products at many Bay Area farmers' markets.

2 large white potatoes

$1/4$ cup lemon-flavored olive oil, such as O or Sciabica

$1 1/4$ cups Seafood Velouté (page 208)

$1/2$ cup heavy whipping cream

2 tablespoons extra virgin olive oil

4 black bass fillets, about 6 ounces each

Kosher salt and freshly ground pepper to taste

3 to 4 ounces osetra caviar

To Drink

Chenin Blanc, Chardonnay

Masa's recommends: 1996 Domaine Des Baumard Chenin Blanc, Savennieres

Cook the potatoes in salted, rapidly simmering water until tender when pierced with a fork, about 20 minutes. Drain. Let cool until they are easy to handle but still warm. Peel the potatoes and place them in a small bowl. Add the lemon olive oil and use a fork to mash the potatoes. Set aside and keep warm.

Combine the fish velouté and cream in a small saucepan and heat over medium-low heat. Meanwhile, heat the olive oil in a large nonstick sauté pan over high heat and sear the bass, skin-side down, until the skin is crispy, about 5 minutes. As it cooks, season the top side with salt and pepper. Turn the fish over and sauté for 2 minutes, or until opaque throughout. Remove from the heat.

Divide the potato between 4 serving plates. Place a fillet of bass on top of each serving. Stir half of the caviar into the hot cream sauce. Spoon the sauce around the fish and potato. Garnish the fish with the remaining caviar and serve immediately.

SERVES 4

MAYA RESTAURANT

Richard Sandoval
Executive Chef

MEXICAN CUISINES—and there are dozens of distinct regional styles, more than you'll find in almost any other country—are among the most delicious, refined, and complex in the world. Yet for decades, Mexican restaurants have concentrated on a limited selection of mostly generic recipes from a limited number of regions, so that many Californians have little sense of the country's true gastronomic diversity. Maya has gone a long way towards offering San Franciscans a deeper taste of Mexico.

Chef and owner Richard Sandoval opened Maya in Manhattan in 1997, and in 1998 brought the concept to San Francisco. He's not an absentee chef, though; he spends time in both his restaurants. Three of Sandoval's brothers work with him in the two-restaurant enterprise. Maya's signature dishes include a remarkable tuna taco, dramatically presented guacamole, and roasted poblanos filled with an exuberant jumble of seafood. The food is not classic Mexican fare, but exciting interpretations informed by traditional ingredients and techniques and Sandoval's inspired creations.

303 SECOND STREET
(415) 543-2928

Tacos de Atún

Traditional tacos consist of a little chopped meat or seafood folded into two hot but not crisp corn tortillas and topped with minced onion, cilantro, and a dollop of salsa. Both the textures and flavors of this appetizer are more complex than those of its humble but delicious cousin.

2 cups pomegranate juice, preferably fresh
4 flour tortillas, 12 inches in diameter
6 ounces jicama, peeled and cut into julienne
6 tablespoons freshly squeezed lemon juice
3 teaspoons honey
Kosher salt and freshly ground pepper to taste
5 tomatoes, peeled, seeded, and diced (see page 218)
6 tablespoons white sesame seeds, toasted (see page 216)
2 chiles de árbol, roasted and ground (see note, next page)
6 tablespoons olive oil or vegetable oil
1 pound ahi tuna, cut into $1/2$-inch cubes
2 teaspoons black sesame seeds, toasted, for garnish (see page 216)

To Drink

Pilsner, lager, Chardonnay
Maya recommends: 1998 Calera
Chardonnay Central Coast

Pour the pomegranate juice into a small nonreactive saucepan and bring to a boil over high heat. Decrease the heat to medium-low and simmer until the liquid is reduced to about $1/3$ cup. Set aside to cool. Cut each tortilla into 6 equal triangles, cover, and set aside.

Toss the jicama with 2 tablespoons of the lemon juice and 1 teaspoon of the honey. Season to taste with salt and pepper. Cover and refrigerate until ready to serve.

To make the tomato sauce, combine the tomatoes, white sesame seeds, the remaining 2 teaspoons of honey, the remaining 4 tablespoons of the lemon juice, and the chiles. Season with salt and pepper and set aside.

Heat the oil in a sauté pan over high heat, add the tuna, and cook, tossing constantly for 1 minute. Add the tomato sauce, bring to a boil, and remove from the heat immediately. Cover to keep hot.

Heat the tortillas in a large dry skillet over medium heat for 2 minutes on each side, until they are just golden brown and barely crisp. Divide the jicama among 4 individual plates, setting it in the middle of each plate. Surround the salad with tortilla triangles and top each triangle with some of the tuna mixture. Drizzle pomegranate reduction over both the salad and the tuna, garnish with the black sesame seeds, and serve immediately.

SERVES 4

Note: Chiles de árbol—literally "chiles of the tree"—come from a busy plant with thick stems; hence their name. These thin two- to three-inch long chiles are harvested when they are ripe and red and sold after they have been dried. They have a slightly smoky flavor. Roast them in a small heavy frying pan over medium-high heat, turning occasionally, until they are fragrant, 5 to 7 minutes. Remove the stems and grind them to a fine powder using a molcajete or mortar and pestle.

Monkey Warner's Cobweb Palace

Of the many San Francisco restaurants that live on in legend, only one of the most intriguing is the Cobweb Palace, located on Meiggs Wharf in North Beach from 1856 to 1897, when its owner, Abe "Monkey" Warner, retired at the age of eighty. The ramshackle eatery, which was apparently not much more than a shed, was packed with Warner's souvenirs from around the world. Overhead was a jumbled canopy of cobwebs, left alone because Warner refused to displace the handiwork of the spiders he so loved. He kept monkeys and tropical birds in cages, and let other animals—cats, dogs, and according to folklore, bears—roam freely through the place as he served up what is said to be freshest seafood of the day.

Mariscada

This extremely simple seafood stew is visually striking with black rice and red sauce. I like to serve a spicy black bean soup as a first course (that way, I have black bean broth for the rice), and end the meal with a refreshing mango or lemon sorbet.

To Drink

Sauvignon Blanc, red ale

Maya recommends: 1998 Joseph

Phelps Sauvignon Blanc Napa

Valley

> 3 tablespoons olive oil
> 8 littleneck clams, scrubbed
> 16 black mussels, scrubbed and debearded if necessary
>   (see page 220)
> 12 bay scallops
> 8 large shrimp, shelled and deveined (see page 219)
> Kosher salt and freshly ground pepper to taste
> Black Rice (recipe follows)
> Red Pepper–Coriander Sauce (recipe follows)
> Fresh cilantro leaves for garnish

Heat 2 tablespoons of the olive oil in a large sauté pan over medium-low heat. Add the clams and mussels, cover, and cook until the shellfish open, 7 to 8 minutes. Discard any that do not open. Heat another large sauté pan over medium-high heat, add the remaining tablespoon of olive oil, and sear the scallops for 2 minutes on each side, or until golden brown. Add the shrimp, season with salt and pepper, toss, and cook for 2 to 3 minutes or until the shrimp turn pink.

To serve, place a generous serving (about 3/4 cup) of black rice in the center of each of 4 plates and surround with the shellfish, arranging it attractively. Drizzle with the sauce, garnish with cilantro leaves, and serve immediately.

Black Rice

> 12 tablespoons (1 1/2 sticks) unsalted butter
> 1 cup long-grain rice
> 2 cups black bean broth (see note, next page)
> 1 ripe plantain, peeled and diced
> Kosher salt and freshly ground pepper

Melt 6 tablespoons of the butter in a medium saucepan over medium-low heat. Add the rice and sauté for 10 minutes, stirring constantly. Add 2 cups of the bean broth and bring to a boil. Decrease the heat to low, cover, and simmer until all of the liquid is absorbed, about 15 minutes. Remove from the heat and let rest for 5 to 10 minutes before removing the lid.

Melt the remaining 6 tablespoons butter in a small sauté pan over medium heat. Add the diced plantain, and cook, tossing frequently, until golden brown. Gently fold into the rice. Season with salt and pepper to taste. Serve warm.

SERVES 4

Note: Black bean broth is the liquid in which black beans have been cooked.

Red Pepper–Coriander Sauce

8 red bell peppers, seeded and deribbed
2 teaspoons coriander seeds, crushed
$^1/_2$ teaspoon sherry wine vinegar
$^1/_2$ teaspoon honey
$^1/_3$ cup olive oil
Kosher salt and freshly ground pepper to taste

Pass the peppers through a juicer. Pour the juice into a small saucepan and bring to a boil over high heat. Decrease the heat to medium-low and simmer until the juice is reduced by three-quarters, about 20 minutes. Stir in the coriander, vinegar, and honey. Gradually whisk in the oil to make an emulsified sauce. Strain through a fine-meshed sieve. Season with salt and pepper.

MAKES ABOUT 1/2 CUP

Mejillones with Watercress and Stuffed Focaccia Strips

One of my favorite ways to prepare mussels is to combine them with tangy Mexican chorizo, as chef Richard Sandoval does here—with an interesting flourish contributed by honey. If you find yourself with a bunch of mussels and some chorizo but no focaccia, don't worry. You can always serve the shellfish with plain garlic bread and even hot tortillas alongside.

Stuffed Focaccia Strips (recipe follows)

$1/4$ cup olive oil

$1/2$ large yellow onion, diced

8 ounces Mexican chorizo, preferably Molinari brand, removed from casing

30 black mussels, scrubbed and debearded if necessary (see page 220)

4 cups Lobster Broth (recipe follows)

$1/2$ cup freshly squeezed lemon juice

$1/4$ cup honey

Kosher salt to taste

$2/3$ cup Salsa Buffalo Picante or other medium-spicy tomato salsa

3 bunches watercress, stemmed, for garnish

To Drink

Beaujolais, Pinot Noir, Merlot
Maya recommends: Dry Creek Valley Reserve Merlot 1997

If you are making the focaccia strips, prepare them first, but do not fry them until the mussels are cooking.

To cook the mussels, heat the olive oil in a large, deep saucepan over medium heat. Add the onion and sauté until tender. Add the chorizo and use a fork to break it up as it cooks. When the chorizo has given up most of its fat, drain all but a little off and return the pan to the heat. Add the mussels, lobster broth, lemon juice, honey, and salt. Cover and simmer until the mussel shells have opened, 7 to 8 minutes. Discard any that do not open.

To serve, divide the mussels among large shallow soup bowls, top with the salsa, and sprinkle with a large handful of watercress sprigs. Ladle broth over the top, filling the bowl about half full. Place a focaccia strip on top of each portion and serve immediately.

SERVES 4

Lobster Broth

5 pounds lobster shells
2 pounds shrimp shells
$1/_2$ cup olive oil
1 pound carrots, peeled and diced
1 stalk celery, diced
2 yellow onions, quartered
2 leeks, white part only, diced
1 pound plum tomatoes, diced
2-inch piece fresh ginger, peeled and minced
3 stalks lemongrass, white part only, cut in half

Preheat the oven to 400°. Place the lobster and shrimp shells on a baking sheet and bake until dried, about 15 minutes. Meanwhile, heat the olive oil in a large saucepan over low heat. Add the carrots, celery, onions, leeks, and tomatoes, and cook slowly until they are tender, 15 to 20 minutes. Add the roasted shells, ginger, lemongrass, and water to cover. Bring to a boil over high heat, reduce the heat to medium-low, and simmer until the liquid is reduced by half, about 20 minutes. Strain through a fine-meshed sieve, pressing on the back of the solids with a large spoon. Pour the strained broth into a clean saucepan, bring to a boil over medium heat, decrease the heat to low and simmer for 10 minutes. (This recipe makes about 4 cups of broth.)

Stuffed Focaccia Strips

Four 1 by 5-inch strips focaccia, sliced in half lengthwise
$1/_4$ cup shredded Gouda cheese
$1/_4$ cup shredded Oaxaca cheese, or shredded mozzarella
2 eggs, beaten
2 cups all-purpose flour
1 cup panko (Japanese bread crumbs)
2 cups olive oil

In a small bowl, toss together the 2 cheeses and then cover the bottom half of each focaccia strip with some of the cheese mix. Cover with the top half of the focaccia. Carefully dip each strip in the beaten eggs and roll it in flour. Dip into the egg a second time and roll it in panko. When ready to serve, heat the oil in a large heavy skillet over medium heat and fry the focaccia strips, turning them once, until they are golden brown. Transfer to absorbent paper to drain.

THE OLD CLAM HOUSE

George Reyes
Chef

THE WORLD WOULD BE seriously impoverished if all the places like the Old Clam House disappeared, leaving nothing in their wake but shiny new eateries, professionally decorated, immaculately maintained, and all too often utterly without character or soul. There aren't many of this ilk left, and it's worth a trip to the warehouse district south of Bernal Heights to indulge in a bit of authentic Old San Francisco dining.

Old license plates line the walls of the bar, and the last time I looked there wasn't a single vanity plate among them. You can't do better than a big bowl of the namesake shellfish, succulent steamer clams redolent with butter and garlic. This is why San Francisco sourdough bread was invented, to soak up these savory juices.

299 BAYSHORE BOULEVARD
(415) 826-4880

Steamers

Few seafood dishes are more satisfying that a bowl of steamed clams with plenty of garlic. A finely honed sauce offers tremendous pleasure and an artistic presentation satisfies our sensibilities on several levels, but sometimes the simplest pleasures are what we crave. That's when I turn to a recipe such as this one. Be sure to sop of the cooking juices with garlic bread; it's almost the best part.

To Drink

Bianco d'Alcamo, Corvo Bianco

Old Clam House recommends:

Chardonnay

$^1/_4$ cup Clarified Butter (page 201)

4 dozen cherrystone clams, scrubbed

$^1/_2$ cup water

6 cloves garlic, minced

$^1/_2$ cup dry white wine

2 tablespoons minced fresh flat-leaf parsley

Hot sourdough bread, sliced

Melt the butter in a small saucepan. Set aside and keep warm.

Put the clams in a large, heavy pot and add the water. Cover and steam until the clams have opened, 8 to 12 minutes. Transfer the clams to 2 large bowls, discarding any that did not open. Add the garlic and wine to the pan liquid and simmer for 2 minutes. Add the parsley and pour the mixture over the clams. Serve immediately, with the butter and bread alongside.

SERVES 2

Open and Closed Case for Freshness

Oysters, clams, mussels, scallops, cockles, conch, and other mollusks must be alive when you purchase them, something you can ascertain by pressing on any open shells or, in the case of univalves, by pressing on the exposed muscle. Living shellfish will close tightly when disturbed, and any extended muscle will retract to the safety of the shell. When you cook live mollusks, the muscle relaxes and the shell automatically opens. Clams, oysters, cockles, and other shellfish that don't open during cooking must be discarded, because they were dead to begin with. Sometimes an unopened shell will be filled with nothing but sand and mud.

Mescalanza

As with almost any seafood stew, the specific shellfish you use here can be varied depending on what is available.

1 bottle (750 ml) white wine

6 cloves garlic, minced

$1/2$ cup (1 stick) butter, chilled

Kosher salt and freshly ground pepper to taste

8 cherrystone clams, scrubbed

4 small to medium oysters, such as Hog Island Sweetwaters

8 black mussels, scrubbed and debearded if necessary
    (see page 220)

4 jumbo shrimp

8 fresh sea scallops, shucked

1 Dungeness crab, cooked, cleaned, and cracked into 4 pieces (see page 220)

2 tablespoons minced flat-leaf parsley for garnish

Toasted Garlic Bread (page 214)

To Drink

Soave Classico, Frescati Superiore, Irish stout

Old Clam House recommends:

Zinfandel

Pour the wine into a large stainless steel pot and bring to a boil over medium-high heat. Cook to reduce to about $1/3$ cup, about 15 minutes. Add the garlic and simmer 1 minute more. Whisk in the butter, 2 tablespoons at a time. Remove from the heat and season with salt and pepper.

Meanwhile, arrange the clams, oysters, mussels, shrimp, scallops, and crab in the basket of a large steamer and add the water. Bring to a boil over high heat, cover, and steam until the clams, oysters, and mussels open, 4 to 6 minutes. Discard any of the bivalves that do not open.

Divide the shellfish among 4 serving bowls. Pour sauce over each portion, garnish with parsley, and serve immediately, with garlic bread on the side.

SERVES 4

Clam House Linguine

The secret to this dish is to cook the fish only until it is just done, so that the flavors remain bright and delicate, the textures moist and tender.

1 pound linguine

Kosher salt

3 tablespoons unsalted butter

10 ounces mushrooms, sliced

8 ounces snapper fillet, boned and diced

12 ounces calamari, cleaned and sliced (see page 219)

Freshly ground pepper to taste

8 ounces bay shrimp

2 cups Marinara Sauce (recipe follows), heated

Cook the pasta in salted boiling water until it is al dente, 9 to 11 minutes. Drain, put in a large bowl, and cover with a tea towel to keep hot.

Meanwhile, melt the butter in a large sauté pan over medium-high heat. Add the mushrooms, decrease the heat to medium, and sauté, stirring frequently, until the mushrooms are limp and give up their liquid, about 12 minutes. Increase the heat to high and add the snapper, calamari, salt, and pepper. Toss thoroughly and cook until the fish turns opaque, 3 to 4 minutes. Add the bay shrimp and heat through. Stir in the warm marinara sauce. Taste and correct the seasoning. Toss the sauce with the linguine, divide among 4 individual bowls, and serve immediately.

SERVES 4

Marinara Sauce

2 tablespoons olive oil

1/2 small onion, diced

3 cloves garlic, minced

Kosher salt to taste

1/2 teaspoon dried oregano

1/4 teaspoon dried thyme

1/4 teaspoon crushed red pepper flakes

³/₄ cup dry white wine
One 14-ounce can crushed tomatoes
1 tablespoon tomato paste
1 tablespoon minced fresh flat-leaf parsley
Freshly ground black pepper to taste

Heat the olive oil in a large frying pan over medium-low heat. Add the onion and cook it, stirring occasionally, until it is limp and fragrant, 7 or 8 minutes. Add the garlic and sauté 2 minutes more. Season with salt. Add the oregano, thyme, and red pepper. Stir in the wine, increase the heat to high, and cook until the wine is reduced by two-thirds, 3 or 4 minutes. Stir in the tomatoes and tomato paste. Reduce the heat to medium and simmer until the sauce is slightly thickened, 12 to 15 minutes. Stir in the parsley and correct the seasoning with salt and black pepper to taste. Store, refrigerated, for up to 2 days. Reheat before using.

MAKES ABOUT 2 CUPS

Happy as a Clam

Can shellfish bring happiness into your life? Well, sort of. Shellfish contain tyrosine, which the brain converts to dopamine and noreprinephrine, two of the body's most powerful "feel-good" chemicals. Sober science will say no more than that these chemicals stimulate mental activity.

So if you want to feel good before a test, eat shellfish. Of course, if you don't have a test, you'll feel even better. Look at it this way: Shellfish are good for your heart and your mind, and that should be enough to make anyone happy.

—Maggie Waldron, *Cold Spaghetti at Midnight*

PINTXOS

Bernat Donés
Executive Chef

CHEF BERNAT DONÉS is from Barcelona, where you'll find some of the most scrumptious seafood on the planet. In the Boqueria, an enormous market in the center of Barcelona, seafood vendors offer everything from baby eels just two inches long to enormous bluefin tuna and dozens of species of fish and shellfish unfamiliar to the American eye and palate. The city is a veritable symphony of seafood, and it is common to see diners tucking into huge platters of raw oysters or shrimp paella at 3 A.M.

San Franciscans don't eat as late as Europeans, but Bernat has dazzled local diners with his exuberant dishes since Pintxos opened its doors in the spring of 1999. Pablo Zubicarary, owner of the restaurant, is from the Basque country, a region also renowned for its seafood cuisine. This highly successful and creative partnership between Bernat and Pablo combines flavors, techniques, and ingredients from both regions. The word *pintxos* (PEEN-choz) means little morsel, or appetizer, and there are plenty on the extensive menu, which also includes excellent vegetarian dishes.

557 VALENCIA STREET
(415) 565-0207

Txangurro (Fresh Dungeness Crab with Sofrito)

If you do not have live Dungeness crab, you can make this dish using lump crabmeat and the scallop shells available in cookware stores.

1 small yellow onion, cut in half

1 bay leaf

2 tablespoons kosher salt, plus salt to taste

4 small live Dungeness crabs

3 tablespoons olive oil

2 red onions, diced

4 tomatoes, chopped

4 cloves garlic, minced

2 tablespoons minced fresh flat-leaf parsley

2 tablespoons unsalted butter

2 tablespoons Scotch whisky

Freshly ground pepper to taste

$1/2$ cup fresh bread crumbs, lightly toasted (see page 217)

4 cups mixed salad greens

2 lemons, sliced, for garnish

To Drink

Albariño, Sauvignon Blanc
Pintxos recommends: Martin
Codax 1999 Albariño, Galicia,
Spain

Fill a large pot two-thirds full with water and add the yellow onion, bay leaf, and the 2 tablespoons salt. Bring to a boil over high heat. Carefully plunge 2 of the crabs into the boiling water and cook for 11 minutes. Transfer the crabs to a sink or colander to drain and repeat with the remaining 2 crabs. Let the crabs cool to the touch. Clean and crack them and remove the meat from the shells (see page 220). Clean the top part of each shell, and set the shells and the crabmeat aside.

Heat the olive oil in a medium sauté pan over medium-low heat, add the red onions, and sauté, stirring occasionally, until very tender, about 15 minutes. Add the tomatoes, garlic, and parsley and cook for 15 minutes. Remove from the heat, stir in the butter, and let cool to room temperature.

Preheat the oven to 350°. Add the crabmeat and whiskey to the cooled vegetables, toss lightly, and season with salt and pepper. Spoon the mixture into the clean crab shells, top with the bread crumbs, set on a baking sheet, and bake for 10 minutes, or until the mixture is heated through. Divide the salad greens among 4 individual plates, set a crab shell on top of the lettuce, garnish with lemon slices, and serve immediately.

SERVES 4

Piquillo Rellenos de Pescado (Piquillo Peppers with Fish, Squid, and Black Sauce)

The *pimiento del piquillo* is grown in the Basque province of Navarra, the southern-most region of the Basque country. After harvesting, the aromatic peppers are roasted over wood fires, peeled, and packed into jars. The piquillo's own juices cover the peppers and nothing else is added. You can sometimes find these peppers in specialty markets. If you can't, the best substitute is a mild, thick-fleshed pepper—there are many varieties—from the farmers' market. Otherwise, use red bell peppers.

1 cup plus 1 tablespoon olive oil

2 yellow onions, diced

2 green bell peppers, seeded, deribbed, and diced

2 cloves garlic, minced

3 cups plus 3 tablespoons Fish Fumet (page 207)

2 tablespoons squid ink (see note, opposite)

1 bay leaf

Kosher salt and freshly ground pepper to taste

1 red bell pepper, seeded, deribbed, and diced

1 pound ripe tomatoes, peeled, seeded, and finely chopped
  (see page 218)

10 ounces rockfish, diced

10 ounces calamari, cleaned and diced (see page 219)

$1/_2$ cup dry white wine

12 canned piquillo peppers, rinsed, drained, and dried,
  or 12 roasted and peeled red peppers (see page 219)

Extra virgin olive oil for brushing

To make the sauce, heat $1/_2$ cup of the olive oil in a medium saucepan set over low heat. Add half of the onions, half of the green bell peppers, and half of the garlic and cook until the vegetables are very tender, about 15 minutes. Add the 3 cups fish fumet, the squid ink, and bay leaf. Increase the heat to medium and simmer for 20 minutes. Remove and discard the bay leaf. Transfer the mixture to a blender and purée until smooth. Strain through a fine-meshed sieve. Pour into a clean saucepan and simmer over medium-low heat until the mixture is reduced by one-third, about 10 minutes. Season with salt and pepper and set aside.

To make the filling, heat $1/2$ cup olive oil in a heavy saucepan over low heat. Add the remaining onions, green bell peppers, garlic, red bell pepper, and tomatoes, and cook, stirring occasionally, until the vegetables are very tender, about 20 minutes. Increase the heat to medium, add the white wine, and simmer for 10 minutes, until the mixture begins to thicken.

Meanwhile, heat the 1 tablespoon olive oil in a nonstick sauté pan set over high heat. Add the diced rockfish and calamari and cook, tossing frequently, for 2 minutes, or until the fish is opaque. Stir into the vegetable mixture and season with salt and pepper. Set aside to cool.

Preheat the oven to 400°. Place the piquillo or bell peppers on a work surface and spoon the vegetable and seafood filling into a pastry bag without a tip. Pipe filling into each pepper and when it is filled, place it in a baking dish. Drizzle the remaining 3 tablespoons of fish fumet over the peppers and bake for 7 minutes. To serve, reheat the sauce and spoon a generous quantity onto each of 4 individual plates. Set 3 stuffed peppers on each plate and brush them lightly with extra virgin olive oil so they glisten. Serve immediately.

SERVES 4 AS AN APPETIZER

Note: Squid ink can be purchased in Japanese and other Asian markets, and often in Italian markets, too.

About Squid

If you shop in Asian seafood markets, you have probably seen the large thick steaks of the giant Humboldt squid *(Dosidicus gigas)*, which can weigh as much as ten pounds or more. The white steaks cut from the squid's thick mantle—are usually put through a tenderizer before they are sold. They can be stewed, sliced and stir-fried, or pounded and sautéed. The taste of giant squid is unremarkable, though it will absorb the flavor of, say, garlic, in much the same way that abalone does. Giant squid cannot be used in place of the smaller squid known as calamari *(Loligo opalescens)*, a different species with a thinner mantle and more delicate flavor.

Esqueixada (Salt Cod with Tomato, Lemon, and Garlic Oil)

In markets throughout the Mediterranean, fillets of salt cod hang from ceilings like colonies of pale bats. In the United States, most county health departments require that salt cod be kept in the refrigerator, so we miss out on these enticing displays. With salt cod out of sight, we often don't realize it's available, so be sure to ask if you can't find it.

To Drink

Sauvignon Blanc, Soave Classico

Pintxos recommends: 1999 Basa Verdejo, Rueda, Spain

6 ounces salt cod

2 small red onions, very thinly sliced

$1/3$ cup cider vinegar

Kosher salt and freshly ground pepper to taste

1 pound tomatoes, peeled, seeded, and finely chopped (see page 218)

8 tablespoons extra virgin olive oil

1 teaspoon freshly ground white pepper

4 tablespoons cooked small white beans, such as navy beans

2 tablespoons pitted black olives

Romesco Sauce (recipe follows)

Juice of 1 lemon

3 tablespoons minced fresh flat-leaf parsley for garnish

Immerse the salt cod in water in a bowl. Cover and refrigerate for at least 36 hours, changing the water every 12 hours. After the third soaking, taste the cod; if it is still salty, soak it in fresh water for 12 hours longer.

Put the onions in a shallow bowl and add the vinegar, salt, and pepper. Let soak for 30 minutes. Drain, rinse in cool water, and drain thoroughly.

Drain the salt cod, break it into small pieces, and put it in a medium bowl. Add the tomatoes, 5 tablespoons of the olive oil, and the white pepper. Toss thoroughly and set aside.

To serve family style, arrange the onions in a loose circle on a large round serving platter. Top with the white beans and drizzle with $1^{1}/_{2}$ tablespoons of the olive oil. Spoon the salt cod and tomatoes on top, scatter the olives over the salad, and top with 3 tablespoons of the romesco sauce. Drizzle with the remaining $1^1/_2$ table-spoons of olive oil and the lemon juice, and sprinkle with the parsley. Serve immediately with the rest of the romesco sauce on the side.

SERVES 4

Romesco Sauce
....

1 pound ripe tomatoes, peeled, seeded, and diced (see page 218)
1 clove garlic
2 red bell peppers, roasted and peeled (see page 219)
$1/_2$ cup hazelnuts, toasted and skinned (see page 218)
$1/_4$ cup cider vinegar
1 cup olive oil or more as needed
Kosher salt and freshly ground pepper to taste

Put the tomatoes, garlic, peppers, hazelnuts, and vinegar in a medium saucepan. Add enough olive oil to fully cover the vegetables. Season with salt and pepper, place over very low heat, and simmer, uncovered, for 30 minutes. Purée the mixture in a blender or food processor. Taste and correct the seasoning. Cover and refrigerate until chilled, at least 2 hours, or up to 3 days. Remove from the refrigerator 30 minutes before serving.

MAKES ABOUT $1^1/_2$ CUPS

PLOUF

Randall Brown
Executive Chef

P LOUF MEANS "SPLASH," the slap of a wave against the shore, and there's something about the way the word evokes the sound itself that resonates with this delightful restaurant, located in the middle of Belden Street (which most people call Belden Lane), a thriving alley that is one of the most European areas in all of San Francisco. Plan to linger, especially on the rare warm night when diners fill outside tables. When it's cold and foggy, as San Francisco so often is, you'll want to score a table near Plouf's corner fireplace.

There are close to half a dozen good restaurants on Belden Lane, something to suit almost any mood and taste, from a funky French bistro and a lively trattoria to a spiffy new Spanish restaurant. At the heart of Plouf's menu are mussels, big bowls of them offered eight ways (my favorite is with bacon and shallots). You'll also find both oysters and clams on the half shell, savory seafood stews, and elegant seafood ravioli.

40 BELDEN STREET

(415) 986-6491

Bourride of Fish and Shellfish

This stew from chef Ola Fendert, who left Plouf in the spring of 2000, shares at least as much with bouillabaisse as it does with a traditional bourride. As with any seafood soup or stew, be sure not to overcook the fish. Pastis is a French aniseed liqueur.

Fish Stock

1 tablespoon grapeseed oil or olive oil
1 yellow onion, diced
2 fennel bulbs, trimmed and diced
4 garlic bulbs, cloves separated and crushed
1 red bell pepper, seeded, deribbed, and diced
5 tomatoes, quartered
$1/_2$ bunch cilantro, stemmed
1 bottle (750 ml) dry white wine
1 cup pastis
5 pounds bones from white-fleshed fish, rinsed
1 tablespoon tomato paste
Kosher salt to taste

To Drink

California or French Chardonnay, Marsanne

Rouille

Half of a 1-pound baguette
1 cup Fish Stock (above)
Pinch of saffron threads
3 egg yolks
2 cups mild olive oil
Cayenne pepper and kosher salt to taste

1 pound very small new potatoes
1 tablespoon kosher salt
1 pound black mussels, scrubbed and debearded if necessary
    (see page 220)
1 pound cherrystone clams, scrubbed
8 ounces bay scallops
8 ounces jumbo shrimp, shelled and deveined (see page 219)

1 pound monkfish fillets, cut into chunks
1 pound sea bass, cut into chunks
12 or 16 large croutons

To make the stock, heat the grapeseed oil in a large saucepan over medium-low heat. Add the onion and fennel, and cook until tender, about 15 minutes. Add the garlic and bell pepper and cook for 2 minutes. Add the tomatoes and cilantro, stir, and cook for 5 minutes. Add the wine and pastis. Increase the heat to high, bring to a boil, decrease the heat to medium-low, and simmer until the liquid is reduced by half, about 20 minutes. Add the fish bones, tomato paste, salt, and water to cover the fish bones. Simmer for 30 minutes. Strain. Transfer the stock to a clean saucepan and simmer until reduced by one-half to two-thirds.

Put the potatoes in a medium saucepan and add water to cover by 2 inches. Add 1 tablespoon salt and bring to a boil over medium heat. Decrease heat to a simmer and cook until the potatoes are tender when pierced with a wooden skewer, about 15 minutes. Drain; set aside and keep hot.

To make the rouille, pull out the soft insides of the baguette and discard the crust or reserve it for another purpose; tear the soft bread into chunks. Pour the stock into a saucepan and add the saffron. Place over high heat and boil to reduce by two-thirds. Put the chunks of bread in a blender. Add the reduced stock and the egg yolks. Pulse several times to blend well. With the machine running, gradually add the oil in a slow, steady stream. Season with cayenne pepper and salt. Transfer to a bowl, cover, and refrigerate for up to 2 to 3 days.

Heat the stock over medium heat. Add the shellfish and fish, cover, and steam until the clams and mussels open, 3 to 4 minutes. Discard any mussels or clams that do not open. Divide the potatoes among large shallow soup bowls. Ladle the fish and shellfish on top and garnish each serving with a generous spoonful of rouille and two croutons. Serve immediately with the remaining rouille on the side.

SERVES 6 TO 8

Mussels Gratinée

This is one of those dishes that is almost impossible to stop eating, especially if you love mashed potatoes (and who doesn't?). It is particularly well suited to a winter night, when there's a fire roaring nearby.

Garlic Butter

9 tablespoons unsalted butter at room temperature
$^1/_2$ cup fresh flat-leaf parsley leaves
2 tablespoons Roasted Garlic Purée (see page 212)
1 teaspoon minced garlic
Juice of 1 lemon
1 anchovy fillet, drained
Kosher salt
Pinch of cayenne pepper

To Drink

Pinot Blanc, Roussanne, Irish stout

Mashed Potatoes

3 medium russet potatoes, about $1^1/_2$
    pounds, scrubbed
2 teaspoons kosher salt,
    plus more to taste
2 tablespoons unsalted butter
    at room temperature
$^1/_4$ cup cream or half-and-half, heated
Freshly ground black pepper to taste

1 small onion, minced
2 tablespoons minced garlic
48 black mussels (about 3 to $3^1/_2$ pounds), scrubbed
    and debearded if necessary (see page 220)
2 cups dry white wine

To make the garlic butter, place the butter, parsley, garlic purée, minced garlic, lemon juice, and anchovy in the work bowl of a food processor, season with salt and the cayenne, and pulse several times until evenly mixed. Transfer all but 1 table-spoon to a small container, cover, and refrigerate.

Oyster Pirates

When oysters flourished in the San Francisco Bay, you could make a lucrative income by stealing them. Among the more famous oyster pirates was a young Jack London, who purchased a sloop and raided oyster beds on moonless nights. He sold his shady harvest to the saloonkeepers along the Oakland side of the Bay. According to *Oysters: A Connoisseur's Guide and Cookbook,* London is said to have made more in a single night's nefarious fishing than in three months' work at a cannery.

To make the mashed potatoes, put the potatoes in a large saucepan and add water to cover by 1inch. Add the 2 teaspoons salt and cook over medium heat until the potatoes are tender when pierced with a fork, about 30 minutes. Drain the potatoes, put them in a medium bowl, and mash them with a potato masher. Add the butter and hot cream. Continue mixing with the potato masher until the potatoes are smooth and creamy. Season with salt and pepper to taste. Cover and keep warm in a very low oven while cooking the mussels.

In a medium saucepan over medium heat, melt the reserved 1 tablespoon garlic butter. Add the onion and cook until tender, about 10 minutes. Add the minced garlic and cook for 2 minutes. Add the mussels and white wine, increase the heat to high, cover, and cook until the mussels open, 7 to 8 minutes. Discard any mussels that do not open. Using tongs or a slotted spoon, transfer the mussels to a bowl, strain the pan liquid, and reserve it to make soup or sauce.

Let the mussels cool to the touch. Remove the top half of each shell, leaving the mussel in the bottom half.

Preheat the broiler. Spread about $1/2$ teaspoon of the reserved garlic butter on top of each mussel. Divide the mashed potatoes among 4 ovenproof plates and place 12 mussels on top of each serving. Place 2 plates at a time under the broiler until the butter is melted, fragrant, and beginning to turn golden brown. Remove from the oven and serve immediately.

SERVES 4

Curried Mussels

Plouf serves mussels prepared several different ways. This version seems to garner the most attention, and for good reason. Although I've enjoyed mussels seasoned with curry spices in the south of France several times, I've never seen a version quite like this one. The apples add a layer of sweetness, and coconut milk and cream contribute a voluptuousness that is all but irresistible. The addition of the searingly hot vinegar—just a splash—is brilliant; its jolt of heat and acid cuts through the richness of the sauce and perks up the palate with each bite.

2 tablespoons butter

$1/_2$ small yellow onion, minced

2 stalks celery, minced

1 Granny Smith apple, peeled, cored, and finely chopped

1 tablespoon Madras curry powder

Pinch of saffron threads

One 14-ounce can coconut milk

$1/_3$ cup heavy cream

Kosher salt and freshly ground black pepper to taste

2 pounds black mussels, scrubbed and debearded if necessary
    (see page 220)

Habanero Vinegar (recipe follows)

2 tablespoons minced fresh cilantro for garnish

To Drink
Sancerre, Riesling, Gewürztraminer

Melt 1 tablespoon of the butter in a medium saucepan over medium-low heat. Add the onion and celery and cook until very tender, about 15 minutes. Add the apple and cook 2 or 3 minutes more, until the apple begins to soften. Add the curry powder and cook 2 minutes more. Add the saffron and stir in the coconut milk and cream. Increase the heat to medium and simmer 3 minutes. Season with salt and pepper. Add the mussels and cook, covered, until the mussels open 4 to 6 minutes. Discard any mussels that do not open. Ladle the mussels into 4 individual bowls and pour sauce over each portion. Drizzle about half a teaspoon of vinegar over the mussels, sprinkle with cilantro, and serve immediately, with the rest of the vinegar alongside.

SERVES 4

Habanero Vinegar

1 fresh ripe habanero chile
1 cup champagne or white wine vinegar

Using a sharp knife, make several lengthwise slits in the chile. Put it in a small glass bowl or jar and pour the vinegar over it. Cover the container with a nonmetallic lid and let sit for 24 hours. Discard the habanero. The vinegar will keep indefinitely.

MAKES 1 CUP

POSTRIO

Mitchell and Steven Rosenthal
Executive Chefs

ALTHOUGH POSTRIO has an international reputation—how could it not, given the celebrity status of its founder, Wolfgang Puck?—its cuisine is genuinely local, shaped in part by the farmers and fishermen of the Bay Area. Postrio's combination of physical grandeur, best illustrated by the magnificent staircase that descends into the main dining room; the skill and talent of executive chefs Steven and Mitchell Rosenthal; and the authenticity of ingredients is a potent mix that has earned the restaurant heaps of national awards and keeps both locals and visitors returning. The food is shaped by Mediterranean and Asian cuisines, probably the two most important influences in early San Francisco. The stylishness of Postrio can be intimidating, but once you're seated, sit back, pay attention (it's one of the best places in the entire city for people-watching), and enjoy the fine seafood and other creations of a staff that clearly stays on top of its game.

545 POST STREET

(415) 776-7825

Italian Fish Soup (Cacciucco)

In Livorno, a coastal city south of Pisa on the Ligurian Sea, fish—usually red mullet—stewed in a thin broth of olive oil and tomato is known as cacciucco and is the inspiration of this more complex version.

To Drink

Pinot Grigio, Pinot Blanc
Postrio recommends: 1998
Zemmer Pinot Grigio, Alto Adige,
Italy

$1/_2$ cup extra virgin olive oil, plus oil for drizzling

3 cloves garlic, very thinly sliced

1 teaspoon red pepper flakes

1 tablespoon tomato paste

$1/_2$ cup dry white wine

16 mussels, scrubbed and debearded if necessary (see page 220)

8 ounces rock shrimp

4 ounces bay scallops, or halved sea scallops

$1 1/_2$ cups Lobster Broth (page 132)

1 tablespoon minced fresh oregano

Kosher salt and freshly ground pepper to taste

Fresh flat-leaf parsley leaves for garnish

Heat the $1/_2$ cup olive oil in a heavy, 8-cup saucepan over medium-high heat. Add the garlic and fry, tossing frequently, until it turns golden brown. Be careful not to burn it. Stir in the pepper flakes, tomato paste, and wine. Add the mussels, shrimp, and scallops. Cover and cook for 2 minutes. Remove the lid, add the lobster broth, and cook over medium-high heat until the liquid begins to thicken, about 5 minutes. Discard any mussels that do not open. Add the oregano, salt, and pepper. Ladle into individual shallow soup bowls. Garnish with parsley, drizzle with olive oil, and serve immediately.

SERVES 4

Sweet Shrimp with Candied Jalapenos
and Carrot-Saffron Sauce

In this intensely flavored and unusual dish, the sweetness of the shrimp is mirrored by both the sauce and the sugar syrup in which the jalapenos are cooked. What makes it all work is the heat of the jalapenos, which adds enough of a counterpoint to the sugar that the dish becomes irresistible rather than cloying.

Carrot-Saffron Sauce

2 cups fresh carrot juice (from about 10 carrots)
3 carrots, peeled and chopped
2 star anise pods
1 cinnamon stick
$1^1/_2$ cups ginger ale
Pinch of saffron threads
2 tablespoons coconut milk
2 tablespoons freshly squeezed lemon juice
Kosher salt and freshly ground pepper to taste

Candied Jalapenos

4 jalapeno chiles, stemmed, seeded, and cut into fine julienne
1 cup Simple Syrup (page 201)
Confectioners' sugar for dusting

$1/_2$ cup (1 stick) unsalted butter
$1/_4$ cup water
$1^1/_2$ pounds medium shrimp, shelled and deveined (see page 219)
Salt and freshly ground pepper to taste
12 to 15 small fresh mint leaves for garnish

To Drink

Dry Riesling, Gewürztraminer
Postrio recommends: 1997 Burclin
Wolf Kabinett Riesling, Pfalz,
Germany

To make the sauce, pour the carrot juice into a small, heavy saucepan and bring to a simmer over medium-low heat. Skim off any foam the forms on the surface.

Meanwhile, combine the chopped carrots, star anise, cinnamon stick, and ginger ale in a medium, heavy saucepan. Bring to a simmer over medium heat and cook until the carrots are very tender, 15 to 20 minutes. Add the hot carrot juice and saffron, and simmer for 5 minutes. Remove and discard the star anise and cinnamon stick. Pour the mixture into a blender and purée until smooth. Transfer to a bowl and add the coconut milk and lemon juice. If the mixture is too thick, thin with a little water. Season with salt and pepper.

To make the candied jalapenos, blanch the jalapenos for 1 minute. Drain, plunge into ice water, and drain again. Dry on tea towels. Heat the simple syrup in a small saucepan over medium-low heat. Add the jalapenos and simmer until tender, about 5 minutes. Using a slotted spoon, transfer the jalapenos to a baking sheet and let cool. Dust lightly with confectioners' sugar.

Melt the butter with the water in a large sauté pan over medium-high heat. Season the shrimp on both sides with salt and pepper, add to the pan, and cook, turning once, until pink and just barely firm, about 3 minutes.

To serve, heat the carrot-saffron sauce over medium-low heat and ladle it into warmed shallow soup bowls. Divide the shrimp among the bowls, garnish with mint leaves and jalapenos, and serve immediately.

SERVES 4

Brochettes of Calamari with Watercress, Celery, Spinach, and Sherry Vinaigrette

The celery reduction adds an intriguing earthy flavor and refreshing contrast to the grilled calamari and tangy vinaigrette. It is the sort of refined touch that we expect in good restaurants but rarely take time to prepare at home. This recipe from the Rosenthal brothers is easy to prepare in a home kitchen (if you have a juicer), and worth the bit of extra effort required.

8 stalks celery, diced, plus 1 stalk celery, shaved (see page 218)

2 cups celery juice (about 10 stalks)

4 cups loosely packed fresh spinach leaves

6 tablespoons safflower oil

Celery salt to taste (about $1/2$ to $3/4$ teaspoon)

$1^1/_2$ pounds calamari (about 20 bodies without tentacles), cleaned (see page 219)

Kosher salt and freshly ground pepper to taste

2 cups stemmed watercress

Leaves from 1 head of frisée lettuce

Sherry Vinaigrette (recipe follows)

Combine the diced celery and celery juice in a small saucepan over medium heat and simmer until the celery is tender, about 10 minutes. Strain through a fine-meshed sieve, reserving both the liquid and the celery. Blanch the spinach in salted boiling water for 1 minute. Drain thoroughly, squeezing to remove all liquid. Combine the spinach and cooked celery in a blender or food processor and pulse until smooth. With the machine running, gradually add the safflower oil. Add the celery salt and set aside.

Heat a stovetop grill pan over high heat. Thread the calamari on 8 wooden skewers. Season the calamari on both sides with salt and pepper. Grill on one side for 1 minute, then turn and grill 30 seconds on the second side, or until opaque and lightly browned.

Divide the watercress, shaved celery, and frisée evenly among 4 serving plates. Arrange the calamari on top and spoon some of the vinaigrette over it. Drizzle with the celery reduction and serve immediately.

SERVES 4

Sherry Vinaigrette

6 tablespoons olive oil

5 strips bacon, cut into thin crosswise strips

3 shallots, thinly sliced

$1/4$ cup sherry vinegar

$1/2$ cup dry sherry

6 tablespoons veal demi-glace (see page 210)

2 teaspoons black truffle oil

2 teaspoons whole-grain mustard

Heat 2 tablespoons of the olive oil in a medium, heavy saucepan over medium heat. Add the bacon and shallots and sauté until golden brown. Add the sherry vinegar and simmer to reduce by half. Add the sherry and reduce by half. Stir in the demi-glace and simmer until thick. Let cool to room temperature. Whisk in the truffle oil and remaining 4 tablespoons olive oil. Store leftover vinaigrette in an airtight container for up to 3 days. To use, warm over medium-low heat.

MAKES ABOUT $3^1/4$ CUPS

RED HERRING

Sean Mindrum
Executive Chef

THE LOMA PRIETA EARTHQUAKE of October 1989 influenced seafood in San Francisco more than most people realize. Federal disaster funds paid for construction at Pier 45 at Fisherman's Wharf. Today, seafood distribution at the pier is a thriving industry. When the damaged Embarcadero freeway was demolished, the view from Red Herring—at that time, still Bistro Roti—opened onto newly planted palm trees, the Bay, and the bridge. There are few more fitting spots for a seafood restaurant. Red Herring blossomed under its first chef, James Ormsby, whose international travels shaped the menu. In the spring of 2000, Ormsby moved on and the restaurant enlisted Bruce Hill to take command until Sean Mindrum came on board in June.

The menu here changes twice each season. In the winter months, about a third of all the restaurant's seafood comes from local waters; less is available in the warmer months. At lunch, the menu focuses on simple dishes geared towards the restaurant's many Financial District and downtown clientele. At night, Red Herring's kitchen becomes more adventurous, with interesting preparations of unfamiliar seafood. One of the most popular dishes is tandoori snapper, prepared and served with the bones in place, a technique that results in a more flavorful and more tender fish than one that has been boned before it is cooked.

155 STEUART STREET

(415) 495-6500

Griddled Halibut with Broccoli Rabe and Romesco Sauce

Broccoli rabe has a pleasantly bitter flavor that takes a bit of getting used to if you are unfamiliar with it. Here, rich halibut and spicy-sweet romesco sauce provide excellent contrasts. It is an outstanding dish if you want to introduce someone to this traditional Italian vegetable that has become extremely popular in the United States over the last decade.

3 bunches broccoli rabe (rapini)

9 cloves garlic, minced

$1/4$ cup extra virgin olive oil

$1\,1/2$ teaspoons red pepper flakes

6 halibut steaks

Kosher salt and freshly ground pepper to taste

Romesco Sauce (recipe follows)

6 lemon wedges for garnish

Cook the broccoli rabe in a large pot of salted boiling water until just barely tender, 4 to 5 minutes. Drain thoroughly, then place in a large bowl. Add the minced garlic, olive oil, and pepper flakes. Set aside to cool.

Heat a large nonstick sauté pan over medium-high heat. Season the halibut on both sides with salt and pepper and sear for 3 to 4 minutes on each side, or until golden brown on the outside and opaque throughout.

To serve, spread a layer of romesco sauce on each of 6 dinner plates, place some of the broccoli rabe on top, and place a halibut steak on top of the broccoli rabe. Garnish each serving with a dollop of sauce and a lemon wedge, and serve immediately.

SERVES 6

Romesco Sauce

2 tablespoons olive oil

1 yellow onion, diced

9 cloves garlic, minced

$1/4$ cup blanched almonds

Red pepper flakes to taste

6 red bell peppers, roasted and peeled (see page 219)

4 large plum tomatoes, roasted, peeled, and seeded (see page 218)

$1/2$ cup extra virgin olive oil

Salt and freshly ground pepper to taste

Heat the 2 tablespoons olive oil in a small sauté pan over medium-low heat and cook the onion, stirring occasionally, until it is very tender, about 15 minutes.

Combine the onion, garlic, almonds, and pepper flakes in a blender or food processor and pulse until smooth. Add the roasted peppers and tomatoes. Pulse briefly. Add the $1/2$ cup extra virgin olive oil, and pulse until smooth. Transfer to a small bowl and season with salt and pepper.

MAKES ABOUT $1^{1}/_{2}$ CUPS

Monkfish Osso Buco

Osso Buco is traditionally made with veal shanks, braised slowly and served over saffron risotto or creamy polenta and topped with minced lemon zest and parsley. Monkfish prepared in a similar fashion is outstanding because the fish is sturdy enough to stand up to the style of cooking.

To Drink

Chianti Classico, Barbera, Vino Nobile di Montepulciano

Red Herring recommends: Lucca Albate Barbera D'Alba, Piedmont, Italy

Gremolata

$1/_2$ cup minced fresh flat-leaf parsley
3 tablespoons minced fresh lemon thyme or regular thyme
1 tablespoon minced lemon zest
Kosher salt and freshly ground pepper to taste

1 cup all-purpose flour
Kosher salt and freshly ground pepper to taste
One 3-pound piece monkfish, peeled and cut into $2\,1/_2$-inch-thick crosswise pieces
$1/_4$ cup olive oil
2 cups diced carrots
2 cups diced inner celery stalks and leaves
4 cups diced yellow onions
9 cloves garlic, minced
2 cups medium-bodied dry red wine
3 bay leaves
3 cups Lobster Broth (page 132) or Fish Fumet (page 207)
3 cups Veal Stock (page 209) or Beef Stock (page 210)
3 tablespoons butter
Creamy Polenta (page 213)

To make the gremolata, combine the parsley, thyme, and lemon zest in a small bowl. Season with salt and pepper to taste. Cover and set aside.

Season the flour with salt and pepper, dredge the fish in it, and set the fish aside.

Heat the olive oil in a large sauté pan over high heat until the oil is very hot but not quite smoking. Carefully add each piece of monkfish to the pan and brown it on all sides. Transfer the fish to a platter and decrease the heat to low. Pour out half the oil. Add the carrots, celery, onions, and garlic, and cook, stirring occasionally, until very tender, about 15 minutes.

Increase the heat to medium, add the red wine and stir to scrape up the browned bits from the bottom of the pan. Add the bay leaves, broth, and stock, and bring to a simmer. Decrease heat to low. Return the fish, along with any juices that have collected on the platter, to the pan. Cover and simmer over low heat until the fish is completely tender but still attached to the bone, about 30 minutes.

Transfer the fish to a serving platter. Add the butter to the pan and swirl until it is melted. Pour the sauce over the fish, sprinkle the gremolata on top, and serve immediately over the polenta.

SERVES 4

Yucatán Fish Tacos with Cabbage Salsa

One of the best fish tacos I've ever tasted was in La Paz in Baja California, at a tiny taco cart near downtown. It couldn't have been simpler: a few chunks of sautéed rockfish wrapped in two soft corn tortillas and drizzled with a little lime juice and salsa. Former Red Herring chef Bruce Hill's are slightly more complex, but the secret of success remains the same: Use the freshest fish available and cook it quickly. The cabbage salsa is really more of a tangy coleslaw, but regardless of what you call it, it is perfect with the boldly seasoned fish.

To Drink

Negro Modelo, Mexico; margaritas Red Herring recommends: Caipirinha (Brazilian margarita with rum, lime juice, and cane sugar)

2 ounces achiote paste
$1/4$ cup freshly squeezed lime juice
2 tablespoons grated orange zest
1 tablespoon packed brown sugar
$1/2$ cup fresh cilantro leaves
$1/4$ cup extra virgin olive oil
2 pounds fresh rockfish, halibut, snapper, or cod fillets,
**   cut into 2-inch strips**
16 fresh corn tortillas
Cabbage Salsa (recipe follows)

Combine the achiote, lime juice, orange zest, brown sugar, and cilantro in a blender or food processor and pulse to blend. With the machine running, gradually add the olive oil to make a smooth marinade. Put the fish in a medium bowl, pour the marinade over it, and toss lightly to coat throughout.

Heat the tortillas on a medium-hot griddle, turning them frequently, until they are very soft. Wrap in a tea towel to keep warm.

Heat a medium sauté pan over medium-high heat, and cook the fish for about 2 to 3 minutes, tossing continuously, until it is opaque throughout. To make the tacos, set two tortillas, one of top of the other, on a plate, top with some of the fish and some of the cabbage salsa, and repeat until all of the fish and all of the tortillas have been used. Serve immediately.

SERVES 4

Cabbage Salsa

2 cups (about 8 ounces) shredded savoy cabbage

2 carrots, peeled and finely chopped

8 red radishes, finely chopped

1 bunch green onions, white and pale green parts only, cut into thin rounds

1 red bell pepper, seeded, deribbed, and finely chopped

1 jalapeno chile, minced

$1/4$ cup minced fresh cilantro

$1/4$ cup freshly squeezed lime juice

2 tablespoons rice vinegar

Kosher salt and freshly ground pepper to taste

In a medium bowl, toss together the cabbage, carrots, radishes, green onions, bell pepper, jalapeno, and cilantro. Pour the lime juice, vinegar, and olive oil over the mixture and toss again. Season with salt and pepper. Let sit for 1 hour before serving.

MAKES ABOUT 2 CUPS

ROSE PISTOLA

Erik Cosselmon
Executive Chef

DURING HER HEYDAY, Rose Evangelista was one of the most notorious characters in North Beach. Rose was born in San Francisco in 1908 and at age nineteen eloped with a young man who delivered fish and died young when his truck plunged off Highway 1. Eventually, Rose married Fred Evangelista and adopted his nickname of Pistola (after the pistol he had brandished at a local cook) as her last name and the name of the restaurant the couple opened in the early 1950s. Both her temperament and her cooking became legendary. As Reed Hearon planned his North Beach eatery, he contacted Rose for permission to name it after her. Rose died in 1998, at the age of ninety, but she lives on in the lively eatery just around the corner from the infamous Pistola's, where Rose reigned as the feisty Queen of North Beach for decades. Rose Pistola was voted Best New Restaurant in America in the prestigious James Beard Awards. Hearon was named Chef of the Year in 1996.

532 COLUMBUS STREET
(415) 399-0499

Grilled Sardines with Salsa Verde

Although fresh sardines are very popular throughout the Mediterranean, they haven't quite caught on in the United States, where most people still think of them as nothing more than bait. You'll find them in restaurants all over San Francisco, though, including Rose Pistola. San Francisco diners tend to be both adventurous and sophisticated. After you've had fresh sardines once, you'll understand why they are so popular.

$1/_2$ slice day-old bread

2 tablespoons red wine vinegar (medium acidity)

2 bunches flat-leaf parsley, stemmed

$1/_4$ cup capers, drained

6 anchovy fillets, drained

6 cloves garlic, minced

$1 1/_2$ cups extra virgin olive oil

4 hard-cooked eggs, finely chopped

Kosher salt and freshly ground pepper to taste

12 fresh sardines

1 lemon, cut into wedges, for garnish

Italian country-style bread for serving

To Drink

Sauvignon Blanc, Soave Classico
Rose Pistola recommends: 1998
Sela & Mosca Vermentino di
Sardegna, La Cala, Italy

Prepare a charcoal fire in an outdoor grill or choose a stovetop grill pan.

Put the bread in a blender or food processor, drizzle with the vinegar, and let sit for about 5 minutes. Reserve a small handful of parsley and add the rest, along with the capers, anchovies, and half of the garlic. Pulse to chop coarsely. With the machine running, gradually add the olive oil. Continue processing until the ingredients are well mixed but not puréed. Transfer to a bowl and fold in the chopped eggs. Season with salt and pepper. Set the sauce aside.

Mince the reserved parsley. Place the sardines in a single layer on a baking sheet or large platter and season on both sides with salt, pepper, minced parsley, and the remaining garlic. Grill over medium-hot coals or on a grill pan heated over medium-high heat until opaque throughout, 3 to 4 minutes per side. Transfer to a serving platter, drizzle with a little of the sauce, and garnish with lemon wedges. Serve immediately, with the remaining sauce and the bread alongside.

SERVES 6

Spaghetti with Fresh Sardines

This recipe was inspired by a trip Erik Cosselmon, Rose Pistola's chef, made to Liguria, that beautiful coastal region of northwest Italy, in 1998. Cosselmon uses the technique of finishing the pasta in the sauce, which infuses each strand with intense flavors and makes it glisten.

To Drink

Soave Classico
Rose Pistola recommends: 1997
Colle di Bardelling Pigato, La
Torrotta, Liguria, Italy

12 ounces dried spaghetti or linguine
2 tablespoons olive oil
1 small white onion, minced
1 teaspoon harissa (see note, below)
6 fresh sardines, pan-dressed
$1/_4$ cup dry white wine
$1/_4$ cup tomato sauce
Kosher salt to taste

In a large pot of salted boiling water, cook the pasta until it has softened but is still hard in the center, about 5 minutes, or half of its normal cooking time.

Meanwhile, heat the olive oil in a large sauté pan over medium-low heat and cook the onion until very tender, about 10 minutes. Stir in the harissa. Add the sardines and cook for about 1 minute. Turn and cook for 2 minutes. Add the white wine, tomato sauce, and 2 tablespoons of the water from the pasta. Drain the pasta, reserving some of the water, and add it to the sauce. Agitate the pan gently and cook, stirring occasionally, until the pasta is tender but not mushy, about 5 minutes. If it seems too dry, add 1 to 2 tablespoons of the pasta water. Season with salt. Serve immediately.

Note: Harissa is a chile paste with garlic, coriander, and caraway. It is available in tubes in specialty markets. Chef Cosselmon uses Le Cabanon, a French brand.

SERVES 6

Whole Striped Bass Roasted in Tomato Sauce

If you do not have a sauté pan large enough to hold the fish in a single layer, you will have to improvise. I recommend a baking dish that is large enough for the fish. Prepare the ingredients as instructed, but sauté the fish one at a time, transferring them to a baking dish after turning them. Then bring the liquid to a boil, pour it over the fish, and bake in the dish rather than the sauté pan.

3 whole striped bass, about 1 pound each, pan-dressed
Kosher salt and freshly ground pepper to taste
$1/4$ cup olive oil
1 white onion, finely chopped
$1/2$ cup minced fresh flat-leaf parsley
2 teaspoons red pepper flakes, or to taste
5 cloves garlic, minced
1 cup dry white wine
1 cup tomato sauce
1 cup water

To Drink

Dolcetto, Chianti Classico, Sangiovese
Rose Pistola recommends: 1998 Piani Noce Dolcetto Paruzzo, Italy

Preheat the oven to 475°. Season the fish inside and out with salt and pepper.

Heat the olive oil in a large ovenproof sauté pan over medium-low heat. Add the onion, parsley, pepper flakes, and garlic. Cook, stirring occasionally, until the onion is very tender, about 10 minutes. Move the vegetables aside and add the fish to the pan. Cook for 2 minutes on each side, shaking the pan all the while so that the fish does not stick. Add the white wine, tomato sauce, and water. When the liquid comes to a boil, transfer the pan to the oven and cook, basting the fish with the liquid 2 or 3 times, for 3 minutes, or until opaque throughout.

Serve directly from the sauté pan or carefully transfer to a large, wide bowl. Serve immediately.

SERVES 6

THE SLOW CLUB

Sante Salvoni
Executive Chef

By DAY, THE SLOW CLUB is home to public television and radio personalities and their special guests from the nearby offices of KQED, Inc. All you need to do is stretch your neck a bit to find out what Michael Krasny, host of *Forum*, KQED-FM's popular public affairs program, is enjoying for lunch. By night, the club is transformed into a moody, sultry lounge with fare that executive chef Sante Salvoni describes as contemporary comfort food.

Sante grew up in Cape Cod, where he was influenced by both New England's abundant seafood and his parents' European roots. He's had no problem adapting to the California seasons; you'll find wild king salmon, day-boat scallops, and halibut from Alaska featured on the Slow Club's menu. The recipes themselves may be modern, or they may harken back to Sante's childhood, when his father prepared favorite dishes from his own youth.

2501 MARIPOSA STREET

(415) 241-9390

Chipotle-Glazed Shrimp
with Radish-Cucumber Relish

You must take certain precautions when you prepare and use this powerful glaze. If you've ever worked with chipotles, you already know they can be extremely hot. To remove the stems, you'll need to poke through the sauce and pull out each chipotle, covering your fingers with hot oils in the process. If you are particularly sensitive, wear latex gloves; also consider reducing the quantity of chipotles by half. And even if you're not overly sensitive, wash your hands thoroughly afterwards. When you cook and purée the glaze, do not stand directly over the pan or blender and do not breathe in the aromas, which can sear your nose and throat. That said, the delicious smoky flavor and seductive heat of chipotles make these precautions a very small price to pay. You can use this glaze with almost any grilled fish; it is also delicious with grilled chicken and slow-roasted pork.

Chipotle Glaze

2 cups freshly squeezed orange juice
1/2 cup cider vinegar
1/4 cup honey
2 garlic cloves
One 7-ounce can chipotles in adobo sauce, stemmed
1 tablespoon ground cumin
Kosher salt and freshly ground pepper to taste

Shrimp

1 pound jumbo shrimp, shelled and deveined (see page 219)
1/4 cup fresh orange juice
1 tablespoon minced fresh cilantro
1/4 cup olive oil
Kosher salt and freshly ground pepper to taste

To Drink

Pale ale

The Slow Club recommends: Sierra Nevada pale ale; Anchor Steam beer

Relish

1 English (hothouse) cucumber, peeled, seeded, and thinly sliced
1 bunch (about 8) radishes, thinly sliced
2 tablespoons minced fresh cilantro
Juice of 1 lime
2 tablespoons olive oil
Kosher salt and freshly ground pepper to taste

Prepare the glaze at least 1 day in advance. Combine the orange juice, vinegar, honey, and garlic in a small nonreactive saucepan. Bring to a simmer over medium-high heat and cook to reduce by half, 15 to 20 minutes. Add the chipotles and cumin. Decrease the heat to very low and simmer for 1 hour, stirring occasionally and adding water if the mixture becomes too thick. Remove from the heat and purée in a blender. Season with salt and pepper. Cover and refrigerate at least overnight or up to 4 days.

To prepare the shrimp, toss them with the orange juice, cilantro, and olive oil in a medium bowl. Cover and refrigerate for at least 30 minutes or up to 24 hours.

Soak 12 wooden skewers in water for 1 hour; drain. Prepare a fire in a charcoal grill or heat a stovetop grill pan over high heat. Clean the grilling surface thoroughly and brush it lightly with olive oil. Season the shrimp with salt and pepper. Thread the shrimp on the skewers and grill them on one side for 2 minutes. Turn them over and brush them with the chipotle glaze. Cook for 2 minutes, or until the shrimp are curled and pink. Turn the shrimp again, brush with the glaze, and remove from the grill. Set them aside and keep warm.

In a medium bowl, toss together the cucumber, radishes, cilantro, lime juice, and olive oil. Season with salt and pepper. Divide among 4 individual plates. Arrange shrimp on each portion and serve immediately.

SERVES 4

Grilled Spinach-Stuffed Squid with Salsa Verde

To grill squid tentacles, you'll need to use a grill rack with narrow grids or else the squiggly little things will fall into the hot ashes. Some modern outdoor grills have racks that will work perfectly but others do not, so you might have to improvise. If you don't have a rack that will work, you can heat a heavy pan over the charcoal fire and use it to sauté the squid, or you can use a stovetop grill.

Filling

2 tablespoons olive oil
1 tablespoon minced garlic
6 cups loosely packed spinach leaves
Kosher salt and freshly ground pepper to taste

To Drink

Pinot Noir, Sangiovese
The Slow Club recommends:
Viognier

Salsa Verde

1 tablespoon minced garlic
$1/2$ bunch basil, stemmed
1 bunch flat-leaf parsley, stemmed
2 tablespoons capers, drained
3 tablespoons coarsely chopped cornichons
1 tablespoon red wine vinegar
$1/2$ cup extra virgin olive oil
Kosher salt and freshly ground pepper to taste

$1 1/2$ pounds calamari (about 16), cleaned and peeled (see page 219)
Extra virgin olive oil for coating
Kosher salt and freshly ground pepper to taste

To make the filling, heat the olive oil in a large sauté pan over medium-high heat and sauté the garlic until it just begins to color but is not browned, about 1 minute. Add the spinach, toss, and cook until wilted, about 2 minutes. Season with salt and pepper, transfer to a plate, and let cool to room temperature.

Meanwhile, make the salsa verde. Put the garlic, basil, parsley, capers, cornichons, and vinegar in a blender or food processor. Pulse 2 to 3 times, then process until blended. With the machine running, gradually add the extra virgin olive oil in a thin stream. Transfer to a small bowl, season with salt and pepper, and set aside.

Squeeze the spinach gently to remove excess liquid. Return it to a bowl and toss it with a fork so that it is not too densely packed. Place the squid bodies on a work surface and fill each one with some of the spinach, being careful not to pack the tubes too tightly. Set on a baking sheet, cover, and refrigerate for up to 4 hours.

Prepare a fire in a charcoal grill or heat a stovetop grill pan. Clean the grilling surface thoroughly and brush it lightly with olive oil. Coat the stuffed squid bodies and the tentacles with olive oil and season with salt and pepper. Grill the squid bodies for 2 to 3 minutes, turn, and grill 2 to 3 minutes more, or until the tubes are opaque. Grill the tentacles until they are opaque, about 2 minutes.

Divide the squid bodies among 4 serving plates, drizzle with salsa verde, scatter the tentacles on top, and serve immediately.

SERVES 4

Sea Bass with Apples, Currants, and Warm Frisée Salad

In California, apples begin to ripen in midsummer, when Gravensteins appear. By early fall, there are dozens of heirloom varieties available at farmers' markets throughout the state. If you can't get a variety suggested in this recipe, just ask any apple grower or a knowledgeable produce manager what he or she recommends as a substitute. You want to be sure to use an apple that will not fall apart when it is sautéed.

Vinaigrette

1 tablespoon cider vinegar

3 tablespoons apple cider

1 teaspoon Dijon mustard

$1/4$ teaspoon kosher salt

$1/8$ teaspoon freshly ground black pepper

$1/2$ cup extra virgin olive oil

To Drink

Champagne

The Slow Club recommends:

Sancerre, Pinot Grigio

Sauce

2 tablespoons unsalted butter

2 Braeburn, Sierra Beauty, or Fuji apples, cored and cut into 6 wedges each

2 shallots, thinly sliced

$1/4$ cup dry currants, soaked in hot water for 30 minutes and drained

$1/2$ cup apple cider

$1/4$ cup cider vinegar

4 sea bass fillets, about 6 ounces each

Kosher salt and freshly ground pepper to taste

2 tablespoons olive oil

Leaves from 1 small head frisée lettuce

To make the vinaigrette, combine the vinegar, apple cider, mustard, salt, and pepper in a small bowl. Gradually whisk in the oil and set aside.

To make the sauce, melt 1 tablespoon of the butter in a medium sauté pan over medium-high heat until it foams. Add the apples and sauté, turning frequently, until golden brown on both sides. Add the shallots and currants and sauté until the shallots are translucent, about 3 minutes. Add the apple cider and cider vingar and simmer to reduce by half, about 2 minutes. Drain the sauce into a small bowl. Transfer the apple mixture into a separate bowl and return the cooking liquid to the sauté pan. Simmer over low heat to reduce by half. Whisk in the remaining butter until incorporated. Pour the sauce into a small pitcher, cover, and keep warm until ready to serve.

Season the fish fillets on both sides with salt and pepper. Clean the sauté pan, add the olive oil, and heat over medium-high heat until hot but not smoking. Add the fillets and cook on one side for 4 minutes or until golden brown. Turn the fillets over and sauté for 3 minutes or until golden brown on the second side and springy when pressed gently with your finger. Transfer the fillets to a plate and keep warm.

Return the sauté pan to medium heat, add the frisée, and stir until it begins to wilt. Add the vinaigrette and toss thoroughly. Divide the frisée among 4 individual plates, set a sea bass fillet on top of each portion, and spoon some of the apple-currant mixture on and around the fish. Pour sauce around the edge of the greens and serve immediately.

SERVES 4

STARS

Amaryll Schwertner
Executive Chef

A GOOD TABLE AT STARS was, in the heady 1980s when Jeremiah Tower's star was at its zenith, a score, a symbol of success, a sign of arrival at ground zero of the city's hottest social scene. Tower eventually left the big stage he had created and retreated to the languid comfort of the tropics, where he lived in Manila for several years. After his departure, the partners closed briefly, remodeled, and reopened the restaurant using the same name, a fairly risky move given the notoriety of Tower's tenure.

Christopher Fernandez, who left Stars as this book was going to press, did a superb job. He didn't try to duplicate Stars' flash, but instead offered well-crafted Mediterranean fare genuinely inspired by the seasons. The new Stars caught my eye for the first time when they offered sand dabs with Meyer lemons, two prized local ingredients. Seafood is not a specialty here—meats from the new rotisserie are—but sand dabs have legions of fans, and they will not be disappointed by the kitchen's straightforward preparations for this and other kinds of fish.

555 GOLDEN GATE AVENUE

(415) 861-7827

Roasted Sand Dabs
with Gypsy Peppers and Fennel

Here, chef Christopher Fernandez offers an unusual take on San Francisco's popular sand dabs. Most often, you find these small flat fish fried and served with lemon wedges. In this dish, the sand dabs steam in the savory aromas of the vegetables, released by the water as it evaporates in the oven. Remember that sand dabs have a lot of bones, a characteristic that Americans are growing more comfortable with as we eat more seafood. This dish is best in the late summer and early fall when gypsy peppers are in season.

$1/_4$ cup extra virgin olive oil

2 golden-orange gypsy peppers, yellow bell peppers,
   or red bell peppers, seeded, deribbed, and cut into julienne

2 fennel bulbs, trimmed and cut into julienne

1 red onion, diced

1 teaspoon minced fresh thyme

3 to 4 cloves garlic, thinly sliced

$1/_2$ cup dry white wine

8 whole sand dabs, pan-dressed

Kosher salt and freshly ground pepper to taste

1 cup water

1 lemon, cut in half

2 tablespoons minced fresh flat-leaf parsley for garnish

Preheat the oven to 400°. Heat the olive oil in a large ovenproof sauté pan over medium heat. Add the peppers, fennel, onion, and thyme, and sauté until the peppers are tender but not mushy, 10 to 12 minutes. Add the garlic and wine and cook 10 minutes more. Transfer the vegetables to an ovenproof casserole dish.

Season the sand dabs on both sides with salt and pepper. Place the fish in a single layer on top of the vegetables, pressing them down so that the vegetables partially cover them. Add the water. Transfer the pan to the oven and bake for 15 to 20 minutes, or until the fish flakes easily when pierced with a fork.

Carefully transfer the sand dabs and vegetables to a large serving platter. Squeeze the lemon over all, sprinkle with parsley, and serve immediately.

SERVES 4

Rock Cod with
Meyer Lemon Sauce and Escarole

This dish offers an elegant yet simple way to serve a common local fish. Baking the cod in bread crumbs keeps the fish moist and flavorful while Meyer lemons, popular and prevalent throughout California, contribute a pleasant combination of sweetness and tartness.

4 boneless, skinless fillets rock cod (rockfish)
Kosher salt and freshly ground pepper to taste
1 cup fresh bread crumbs, toasted (see page 217)
1 tablespoon minced fresh flat-leaf parsley
3 tablespoons extra virgin olive oil

To Drink

Chardonnay

Meyer Lemon Sauce

1 egg yolk
Juice of 1 Meyer lemon diluted with 1 tablespoon water
1 cup peanut oil
1 teaspoon grated Meyer lemon zest
Salt and freshly ground pepper to taste

1 head escarole, trimmed
2 tablespoons unsalted butter
$1/_2$ cup water
Salt and freshly ground pepper to taste

Preheat the oven to 375°. Season the cod on both sides with salt and pepper. In a small bowl, combine the bread crumbs, parsley, and 2 tablespoons of the oil and toss until the oil is completely absorbed. Brush a baking sheet lightly with the remaining 1 tablespoon olive oil, set the cod on it in a single layer, and pack some of the bread crumbs on top of each fillet. Bake for 8 to 10 minutes, or until the bread crumbs are deep golden brown and the fish is opaque throughout.

Meanwhile, make the lemon sauce. Combine the egg yolk and diluted lemon juice in a blender or food processor. Pulse to blend. With the machine running, gradually add the peanut oil in a very thin stream to make a thick emulsified sauce. Fold in the lemon zest and season with salt and pepper. Taste and thin with a little water or lemon juice if necessary to create a loose texture, like thin mayonnaise. Transfer to a small bowl.

Cut the escarole into large chunks. Melt the butter in a large saucepan over medium heat until it foams. Add the escarole and water. Season with salt and pepper. Cover and cook until the escarole is wilted, 5 to 7 minutes.

To serve, divide the escarole among 4 warmed plates and top with the cod. Spoon the sauce next to the fish and serve immediately, with the remaining sauce on the side.

SERVES 4

Warm Crab Soufflé with Bisque Sauce

Although this recipe is quite involved, it is not difficult—you do not need professional knife skills, for example, but you do need time. I recommend making the bisque sauce the day before. You can also cook the leeks beforehand; just be sure to warm them to room temperature before you make the soufflé. And you will be rewarded with abundant praise when your guests savor the voluptuous soufflé cloaked in its luscious sauce. This dish is ideal on a cold, damp winter evening, perhaps during the holidays, when the California Dungeness crab season is at its peak.

1 large Dungeness crab, cooked, cleaned, and cracked (see page 220)

Bisque Sauce

2 tablespoons olive oil
Shells from crab, above
1 small onion, diced
1 small leek (white part only), diced
1 carrot, peeled and diced
1 stalk celery, diced
One 14$\frac{1}{2}$-ounce can chopped tomatoes, preferably Muir Glen brand
1 tablespoon tomato paste
1 cup dry white wine
1 cup brandy
1 bay leaf
1 sprig thyme
4 cups Fish Fumet (page 207) or Chicken Stock (page 205)
4 cups heavy whipping cream

Crab Soufflé

6 tablespoons unsalted butter
1 leek (white part only), diced
Kosher salt to taste
1 tablespoon water
$\frac{1}{4}$ cup flour
1 cup milk
2 cups Bisque Sauce, above
5 eggs, separated

To Drink
Marsanne, Viognier, dry Champagne

1 teaspoon grated lemon zest
1 teaspoon minced fresh chives
Pinch of cayenne pepper
6 sprigs chervil for garnish

Remove the crabmeat from the shells and set the crabmeat aside; reserve all the shells.

To make the sauce, heat the olive oil in a soup pot over medium-low heat, add the crab shells, and sauté, stirring frequently, for 15 minutes, crushing the shells as they cook. Add the onion, leek, carrot, and celery and sauté for 10 minutes. Stir in the tomatoes, tomato paste, wine, and brandy. Increase the heat to high and bring the liquid to a boil. Decrease the heat to medium and simmer until the liquid is reduced by half, 15 to 20 minutes. Stir the mixture frequently so that it does not stick and burn. Add the bay leaf, thyme, and fish fumet, then bring to a boil over high heat. Decrease the heat to medium and simmer until the liquid is again reduced by half, 20 to 30 minutes. Stir in the cream, decrease the heat to low, and simmer until thick, 35 to 40 minutes. Strain through a fine-meshed sieve. Let cool to room temperature. Set aside to serve now, or cover and refrigerate overnight. Reheat before serving.

To make the soufflé, melt 1 tablespoon of the butter in a small sauté pan over medium-low heat. Add the leek, season with salt, add the water and cook, stirring occasionally, until the leak is very tender, 15 to 20 minutes.

Preheat the oven to 375°. Rub the insides of 6 ramekins or soufflé dishes and dust them with flour. Melt the remaining 5 tablespoons butter in a medium, heavy saucepan over low heat, stir in the flour, and cook for 15 minutes, stirring frequently. Do not let the mixture brown. Whisk in the milk and bisque sauce. Remove from the heat, pour into a medium bowl, and let cool to room temperature.

Whisk the egg yolks until blended. Fold the zest, chives, cayenne, leek, and egg yolks into the sauce. Add the crabmeat, folding it in gently. In a large bowl, beat the egg whites until they form stiff, glossy peaks. Fold them into the soufflé mixture and season with a generous pinch of salt. Spoon the batter into the ramekins or dishes, filling each cup about half full. Bake until the soufflés have risen and are golden on top but still moist inside, about 20 to 25 minutes.

Heat the remaining bisque sauce and pour into small pitchers. Garnish each soufflé with a sprig of chervil and serve immediately with the bisque alongside.

SERVES 6

STRAITS CAFÉ

Chris Yeo
Executive Chef

THE STRAIT OF MALACCA separates western Malaysia from the Indonesian island of Sumatra; its southern waters embrace the island nation of Singapore. The cuisine of this part of the world is a complex patchwork of influences, including Malaysian, Chinese, Indian, Burmese, Thai, and Indonesian. Two of these influences, Malaysian and Chinese, have expressed themselves in a full-flavored, spicy style that has evolved over several centuries and is known as Nonya cuisine, now just being discovered by American tourists and diners. Some of the finest examples of this style of cooking are found at Straits Café, where Chris Yeo presides over a ktchen proficient in its earthy and evocative combination of flavors.

San Francisco may lack the humidity, the street stalls of enticing foods sold late into the night, and some of the indigenous ingredients, but if you've never been to Malaysia or Singapore, Straits Café is an excellent location to begin a journey that you will surely want to continue after your first luscious bite of, say, mussels roasted in a wok, or the best laksa, a wonderful seafood stew, that I've found this side of Kuala Lumpur. The decor of Straits Café is funky and whimsical, and the crowd lively and loud. In the evening, the small bar is packed with people enjoying the restaurant's special cocktails, such as their tasty ginger martini.

330 GEARY BOULEVARD
(415) 668-1783

Salmon Pengang

Red jalapenos are jalapenos that have been left on the plant long enough to ripen. They are a little sweeter than green ones, and sometimes a little hotter, too. In a pinch you can use green jalapenos if they are all you have. You can usually find red ones, along with fresh lemongrass, kaffir lime leaves, and banana leaves in Asian markets.

To Drink

Beaujolais, Pinot Noir

Straits Café recommends: Benton Lane Pinot Noir

About 4 red jalapeno chiles

1 onion, diced

18 cloves garlic, peeled

2 stalks lemongrass (white part only), thinly sliced

$1/4$ cup vegetable oil

5 tablespoons sugar

2 teaspoons salt

2 fresh kaffir lime leaves, cut into julienne

4 large banana leaves

Four 4-ounce salmon fillets, pin bones removed (see page 100)

Combine the jalapenos, onion, garlic, and lemongrass in a food processor and pulse until smooth. Heat the oil in a sauté pan over medium-high heat, add the jalapeno mixture, and sauté, stirring constantly, until fragrant, 4 to 5 minutes. Stir in the sugar, salt, and kaffir lime leaves, reduce the heat to low, and simmer for 5 minutes. Remove from the heat and let cool to room temperature.

Preheat the oven to 400°. Place the banana leaves on a work surface and wipe them clean with a damp cloth. Place a fillet in the middle of each leaf, cover with some sauce, and fold the sides and ends of the leaf over the salmon, securing them with toothpicks. Set each wrapped fillet on a baking sheet and bake until almost opaque throughout, about 20 minutes. Remove from the oven and serve immediately.

SERVES 4

Green Curry with Mussels, Shrimp, and Calamari

You'll need to get several of the ingredients in this rich curry in an Asian market. Galangal, a rhizome similar to ginger, can usually be found fresh in such markets, but if you can't find it, use the bottled galangal imported from Thailand. Likewise, try to find fresh curry leaf, a tree leaf for which there is no substitute; if you can only find it dried, soak the dried leaves in water for 30 minutes before using them. Green curries, which are traditional throughout much of Southeast Asia, have a brighter, tangier flavor than red or yellow curries, or most Indian curries. They are particularly good with seafood. Serve this curry with steamed rice on the side, if you'd like.

4 cloves garlic

1 tablespoon thinly sliced lemongrass

2 onions, diced

7 or 8 jalapeno chiles, stemmed and chopped

2 green bell peppers, seeded, deribbed, and chopped

Four or five $1/8$-inch slices galangal

One 2-inch piece ginger, peeled and sliced

4 curry leaves

$1/2$ bunch cilantro, stemmed

$1/4$ cup vegetable oil

One $14 1/2$-ounce can coconut milk

$1 1/2$ cups water

Kosher salt and granulated sugar to taste

1 pound (about 20 to 25) black mussels, scrubbed
    and debearded if necessary (see page 220)

8 ounces medium shrimp, shelled and deveined (see page 219)

8 ounces cleaned calamari, bodies cut into rings (see page 219)

To Drink

Pinot Blanc, Viognier, dry Riesling

Straits Café recommends: Hiedler Weissburgunder Maximum Pinot Blanc

Combine the garlic, lemongrass, onions, jalapenos, bell peppers, galangal, ginger, curry leaves, and cilantro in a food processor and pulse until evenly minced and nearly smooth. Heat the oil in a large heavy saucepan over medium heat. Add the garlic and jalapeno mixture and sauté, stirring constantly, until fragrant, about 5 to 6 minutes. Stir in the coconut milk and water, bring to a boil, decrease heat, and simmer for 10 minutes. Season with salt and sugar. Add the seafood, cover, and simmer until the mussels open, about 4 to 6 minutes. Divide the curry among individual soup bowls and serve immediately.

SERVES 4 TO 6

Lemak Laksa

"You must have a dish called laksa," a friend insisted when I told him I was going to Malaysia. "It is the most wonderful thing I have ever tasted." On my first day in Kuala Lumpur I found two versions, the sour Asam laksa from Penang, and lemak (curry) laksa from Malacca. I was thrilled when I discovered that Straits Café included lemak laksa on their menu. You'll need to shop for ingredients in an Asian market, of course, but none of the ingredients is hard to find. Laksa can be very spicy, and you should adjust the amount of chile paste you use to suit your preference; the hotter you like your food, the more of the chile paste you should use.

To Drink

Pilsner, lager

1 onion, chopped

12 to 16 (2 ounces) cloves garlic

1 stalk lemongrass, thinly sliced

1 to 2 ounces commercial chile paste

$1/2$ ounce Thai prawn paste

$1/2$ ounce dried shrimp

1 ounce (about $1/4$ cup) shelled
   candlenuts or macadamia nuts

Seven or eight $1/8$-inch slices galangal

$1/3$ cup vegetable oil

One $14 1/2$-ounce can coconut milk

$1 1/2$ cups Chicken Stock (page 205)
   or water, plus more as needed

Kosher salt and granulated sugar
   to taste

8 ounces (about 15) small black
   mussels, scrubbed and debearded if necessary (see page 220)

8 ounces medium shrimp, peeled and deveined (see page 219)

8 ounces bay scallops

8 ounces medium-thin or thin rice noodles

$1/3$ cup cilantro leaves for garnish

1 lime, cut into thin wedges, for garnish

Combine the onion, garlic, lemongrass, chile paste, prawn paste, dried shrimp, candlenuts, and galangal in a food processor and pulse until evenly minced and almost smooth. Heat the oil into a large heavy saucepan over medium heat. Add the garlic mixture and cook, stirring constantly, until the mixture separates from the oil, about 8 to 10 minutes. Stir in the coconut milk and chicken stock. Bring to a boil, reduce the heat to low, and cook gently for 10 minutes. Season with salt and sugar to taste; if the sauce tastes flat, add a little more salt and sugar until it perks up. The sauce should be the consistency of soup; if it is too thick, add a little more stock.

Add the mussels, shrimp, and scallops, cover, and cook until the mussels open, about 4 to 6 minutes. Discard any mussels that do not open.

Meanwhile, cook the noodles in a large pot of boiling salted water until just tender. Drain, rinse, and drain again, thoroughly. Divide among large soup bowls. Ladle the laksa over the noodles, garnish with cilantro leaves and serve immediately, with lime wedges on the side.

SERVES 4 TO 6

SWAN OYSTER DEPOT

T HERE WERE ONCE dozens of places like Swan Oyster Depot in San Francisco, fish markets with counters packed with customers savoring raw oysters, cracked crab, and the seafood cocktails, salads, and stews made famous in this seaside city. Today, only Swan, founded in 1912, remains. In 1946, Sal Sancimino bought the company, and today six of his seven children run it. Most of Swan's business is delivering fresh seafood directly to homes throughout San Francisco, a remarkably appealing endeavor in a time when most people purchase food from enormous supermarkets that don't even offer to carry your bags to the car.

Swan is one of the best places anywhere to enjoy fresh seafood, from Olympia oyster cocktails, said to have been invented by a customer decades ago, to the best cracked crab on the planet. A marble counter stretches the length of this colorful institution; eager customers hover along the wall, waiting for a seat to open up. Employees keep up an endless stream of banter, flirting, grousing, telling stories, and shouting as they pop open oysters, pour wine, and scramble around each other in a dizzying whirl of activity. Once you have your own stool, don't let the hungry crowd intimidate you: Take your time, begin with an oyster cocktail, and don't miss the crab, and if you're not sure how to dress it—it comes with a variety of condiments—ask one of the guys to mix up his favorite sauce for you.

1517 POLK STREET

(415) 775-7049

Olympia Oyster Cocktail

If you ask one of the counter guys at Swan Oyster Depot who first came up with their popular Olympia oyster cocktail, you might hear a story about a feisty customer, his name long forgotten, who dumped a dozen or so oysters into a glass of cocktail sauce, slurped it down, and declared he had just invented the oyster cocktail. Soon, oyster bars all over the city were serving their versions. Olympia oysters are tiny, their shells smaller than a quarter, their bodies about the size of a dime; twenty-five of them make a scant one-third cup, or less. Swan goes through a thousand a day, and often more. Olympias are, admittedly, hard to get and even harder to shuck. Read about shucking oysters on page 221, and if you can't get Olympias or don't want to tackle their little shells, make this cocktail with another small oyster, such as Hog Island Sweetwaters, considerably larger than Olympias but still less than a mouthful. (If you make the substitution, you'll need only about two dozen Sweetwaters.)

$2/_3$ cup ketchup

2 tablespoons prepared horseradish

2 tablespoons freshly squeezed lemon juice

Tabasco sauce

80 to 100 Olympia oysters, freshly shucked
   (liquor reserved), and chilled

1 lemon, cut into wedges, for garnish

To Drink
Sauvignon Blanc
Swan recommends: 1998 Honig
Sauvignon Blanc

In a small bowl, mix together the ketchup, horseradish, lemon juice, and a dash of Tabasco sauce. Divide the oysters and their liquor evenly between 4 chilled cocktail glasses or small bowls. Spoon the cocktail sauce on top, garnish with lemon wedges, and serve immediately with Tabasco sauce on the side.

SERVES 4

Squid Salad

....

If you visit Swan's early in the morning, you might be surprised by how many people think an oyster cocktail or a cracked crab makes an ideal breakfast. You might get to watch one of the guys make Swan's popular squid salad, which is simple to prepare at home, too. Opinion is divided as to whether or not a squid's tube-like body needs to be peeled. I like the pale purplish color of unpeeled squid, but I don't like the way the skin sometimes curls away from the flesh, so I often peel it off before cooking. The tentacles, of course, do not need to be peeled.

To Drink

Chardonnay, dry Rosé

Swan recommends: Cuvaison
Chardonnay, Napa Valley

**1 pound small squid, cleaned and peeled, bodies
    cut into 1-inch-wide strips (see page 219)**
$^1/_2$ cup finely chopped white onion
$^1/_2$ cup finely chopped celery
2 cloves garlic, minced
2 tablespoons minced fresh flat-leaf parsley
1 teaspoon anchovy paste
$^1/_4$ cup balsamic vinegar
Salt and freshly ground pepper to taste
$^1/_2$ cup olive oil
1 bay leaf

In a large pot of salted boiling water, blanch the squid rings and tentacles for $1^1/_2$ to 2 minutes, or until opaque. Drain, plunge them into ice water, and drain again. Put the squid in a medium bowl, cover, and refrigerate until chilled, about 1 hour.

In a small bowl, toss together the onion, celery, garlic, and parsley. Mix in the anchovy paste and balsamic vinegar. Season with salt and pepper. Stir in the olive oil. Pour the dressing over the squid, add the bay leaf, and toss thoroughly. Cover and refrigerate for at least 30 minutes or up to 1 hour. Remove the bay leaf before serving.

SERVES 2 TO 4

Crab Louis

You can find more elaborate versions of this classic salad, but Jim Sancimino explains that traditionally, there were just three ingredients: iceberg lettuce, Dungeness crab, and Louis dressing. The iceberg lettuce is crucial; its crisp, clean flavor provides an appealing and necessary contrast to the rich crab without contributing a lot of other flavors that might compete with it. This is definitely not the time to use mesclun or other flavorful heirloom greens.

2 Dungeness crabs, cooked, cleaned, and cracked
    (see page 220)
1$^1/_2$ cups mayonnaise
$^1/_2$ cup tomato ketchup
2 tablespoons minced black olives
2 tablespoons sweet relish
2 tablespoons minced white onion
1 hard-cooked egg, minced
Kosher salt and freshly ground pepper to taste
1 head iceberg lettuce, cored and chopped
1 lemon, cut into wedges

Pick the crabmeat from the shells, keeping the leg meat separate from the body meat. Set it aside.

In a medium bowl, mix together the mayonnaise, ketchup, olives, relish, onion, and egg. Season with salt and pepper.

Divide the lettuce among 4 serving plates and scatter the crabmeat, reserving the 8 leg sections, on top. Spoon the dressing over the crab and place 2 leg sections on each portion. Garnish with lemon wedges and serve immediately.

SERVES 4

TADICH GRILL

Fritz Braker
Executive Chef

You've gotta love a restaurant that started out in a tent back in 1849. After nearly a century on Clay Street, Tadich moved to its current location in 1967. Even with the move, Tadich Grill is steeped in the history of old San Francisco. Some dishes, such as deviled crab, poached salmon, lobster Newberg, crab Louis, and prawns and crab à la Monza, a shellfish stew in a heavily seasoned béchamel sauce served over rice, have been on the menu almost since the beginning. Compared to many of today's pristine preparations and labored presentations, these dishes seem to come from a long-forgotten era, but in fact they remain on the menu because they are enormously popular.

One of the most satisfying meals here can be had at the counter. Simply ask the waiter what fish is freshest, have it grilled or fried, and be sure to get some of the Tadich's legendary tartar sauce alongside.

240 California Street
(415) 391-1849

Tadich Grill's Dungeness Crab Cakes

There are nearly as many versions of crab cakes as there are chefs. This classic version highlights the flavor of the crab, which can be accented with marinara sauce, Creole sauce, curry sauce, tomato-basil sauce, or rémoulade, if you like. Here the crab cakes are served neat, with just a squeeze of lemon.

Béchamel Sauce

1 tablespoon unsalted butter

1 tablespoon flour

1 cup milk

Kosher salt and freshly ground white pepper to taste

2 tablespoons unsalted butter, plus more as needed

1 cup minced shallots

$1/_2$ cup finely chopped celery (2 to 3 stalks celery)

3 cloves garlic, minced

Kosher salt and freshly ground white pepper to taste

1 pound fresh lump Dungeness crabmeat, picked over for shells

1 teaspoon minced fresh basil

2 eggs

1 cup fresh bread crumbs, lightly toasted (see page 217)

Lemon wedges for garnish

To make the sauce, melt the butter in a small saucepan over low heat. Add the flour and stir constantly for 2 to 3 minutes; do not let the flour brown. Gradually whisk in the milk and cook, stirring frequently until the sauce is thick and creamy, 4 to 5 minutes. Season with salt and pepper, remove from the heat, and cool slightly.

Melt 1 tablespoon of the butter in a small sauté pan over medium-low heat and sauté the shallots, celery, and garlic for about 3 minutes, or until the shallots are translucent. Season with salt and pepper, transfer to a large bowl, and let cool to room temperature. Add the crabmeat, basil, eggs, and béchamel sauce, and mix together. Form the mixture into 8 equally sized cakes. Dip the cakes in the bread crumbs and set aside.

Melt the remaining 1 tablespoon butter in a large sauté pan over medium heat until it foams. Add 4 of the crab cakes and cook for 2 to 3 minutes. Turn and cook on the second side until lightly browned, about 2 minutes. Transfer to a plate and keep warm in a low oven while cooking the remaining 4 crab cakes, adding more butter to the sauté pan if necessary.

Place 2 crab cakes on each of 4 individual plates. Garnish with lemon wedges and serve immediately.

SERVES 4

Seafood, Season by Season

As is true with almost everything we eat, most seafood has a season when it is at its best. With the increasing prevalence of aquaculture, fewer people, including chefs, understand seafood seasonality, even though foods eaten at the peak of their true season are almost always better than at other times. Here is a list of seasonal seafood from the Bay Area:

Fall: Lingcod, chum salmon, opah, rockfish, flatfish, swordfish, thresher shark, clams, mussels, squid.

Winter: Dungeness crab, raw oysters, petrale, steelhead salmon, sturgeon, spiny lobster, Monterey prawns, clams, mussels, swordfish.

Spring: Herring, herring roe, raw oysters, bay scallops, squid, Pacific halibut, sardines, anchovies, mackerel, clams, mussels, squid, Santa Barbara spot prawns.

Summer: King salmon, tuna, halibut, white sea bass, oysters for grilling, squid.

Year-round: Local rockfish, sand dabs, farmed catfish, farmed oysters, farmed trout, farmed salmon.

Hangtown Fry

Tadich Grill's Hangtown Fry is really a frittata, a flat omelet that is turned rather than folded.

> **2 slices bacon**
> **$1/_2$ cup fine bread crumbs, seasoned and toasted (see page 217), or flour seasoned with salt and pepper**
> **6 oysters, shucked (see page 221)**
> **1 tablespoon unsalted butter**
> **3 eggs, lightly beaten**
> **3 or 4 shakes Tabasco sauce**
> **Kosher salt and freshly ground pepper to taste**

Fry the bacon in a nonstick sauté pan over medium heat until crisp. Transfer to absorbent paper to drain. Meanwhile, put the bread crumbs in a small bowl, add the oysters, and toss until each oyster is evenly coated. Remove the oysters from the bowl and shake each one to remove any excess coating.

Pour off the bacon fat. Add the butter to the pan and melt over medium heat. Add the oysters and sauté for about $1^1/_2$ minutes on each side, or until the oysters just plump up. Crumble the bacon into pieces and toss it with the oysters. Pour the eggs into the pan. Season with Tabasco sauce, salt, and pepper, and cook until the eggs are almost set, lifting the edges of the cooked eggs to let the uncooked eggs run under them.

Carefully flip the fritatta over and cook for about 2 minutes or until cooked on the bottom. Transfer to a plate and serve immediately.

SERVES 1

Hangtown Fry

For years, the city of Placerville in the heart of the Gold Country was known as Hangtown because of three gold thieves who were hanged there in 1849. Today, no one seems to know the exact origin of its namesake recipe, though two tales are heard most often. In one, a miner who has just struck it rich asks a cook to make him the most expensive dish he can; eggs, oysters, and bacon were the priciest ingredients on hand. Another account credits a condemned prisoner who requests the concoction as his last meal, thus delaying the hour of his death because the ingredients could not be gotten quickly. There *is* agreement on what exactly the dish was: scrambled eggs with oysters and bacon. Over the decades, restaurants have developed their own variations, including the one from Tadich Grill, which is more of a frittata than a scramble.

Pan-Fried Sand Dabs

Fervent sand dab aficionados prefer simple recipes such as this one, served at Tadich Grill for well over a century, in which the unique flavor and texture of the fish is not eclipsed by other ingredients.

To Drink

Sauvignon Blanc

3 $\frac{1}{2}$ to 4 pounds sand dabs, pan-dressed
Flour seasoned with salt and pepper for dredging
Olive oil for frying
1 lemon, cut into wedges, for garnish
4 small sprigs flat-leaf parsley for garnish

Dredge the fish in the seasoned flour.

Pour enough olive oil into a large nonstick sauté pan to just coat the bottom. Heat over medium heat, add fillets in a single layer, and cook for 4 minutes on one side or until golden brown. Turn and cook 4 minutes on the second side, or until golden brown. Transfer to a warm platter and keep warm in a low oven. Repeat to cook the remaining fillets, adding more olive oil to the pan as necessary.

Transfer the sand dabs to individual plates, garnish with lemon wedges and parsley, and serve immediately.

SERVES 4

ZARZUELA

Lucas Gasco
Chef and Owner

WHEN ZARZUELA OPENED in August of 1994, its success was so instantaneous that it was almost immediately impossible to get a table without waiting an hour or more. It quickly became a destination for chefs on their nights off, and one of the best-known chefs in San Francisco could name no other restaurant where he liked to eat—he loved Zarzuela that much. At the time, it was pretty much the only game in town if you wanted real Spanish tapas, those little dishes of intensely flavored foods you find in bars and cafes throughout much of Spain. Today there are several options, and although the lines don't often stretch around the block, Zarzuela remains one of the city's best and most popular neighborhood eateries.

Chef and owner Lucas Gasco may be from landlocked Madrid, but he has an excellent way with seafood. Twice a week, on Tuesday and Thursday mornings, he heads to the fish market at Pier 33, selecting local anchovies, spot prawns, squid, Delta crayfish, and, occasionally, gooseneck barnacles, for the evening's specials. When they're available, minuscule boccarini, teeny deep-fried whole fish, are an ethereal delight. Zarzuela's paella is authentic, full of complex flavors and contrasting textures. My favorite dishes, though, are the fresh sardines sautéed in butter and garlic, and the Pulpo à la Gallega, Zarzuela's sensational octopus, included here.

2000 HYDE STREET
(415) 346-0800

Zarzuela de Pescado y Marisco (Seafood Stew)

The complex flavors in this fragrant stew come from slowly cooked vegetables, spices, brandy, and sherry, each of which contributes its own layer of flavor. The specific seafood, however, is not as crucial and you should feel free to use whatever you have available in your area. If you don't have crayfish or small crabs, for example, use more prawns or add some rock shrimp; use all clams or all mussels, and if you can't get calamari, don't worry about it.

To Drink

Pinot Noir, Pinot Nero

Zarzuela recommends: David Bruce Pinot Noir, Central Coast

Picada

2 cloves garlic

Pinch of saffron threads

6 hazelnuts, blanched and toasted (see page 216)

$^3/_4$ cup olive oil

1 large leek, including pale green parts, washed and diced

1 clove garlic, minced

1 carrot, peeled and diced

2 stalks celery, diced

2 bay leaves

Kosher salt and freshly ground pepper to taste

$1^1/_2$ pounds tomatoes, peeled and quartered (see page 218)

1 pound crayfish

$^1/_2$ cup brandy

6 cups Shellfish Stock (page 208) or Fish Fumet (page 207)

$1^1/_2$ pounds monkfish, grouper, or other firm-fleshed fish fillets, cut into pieces

$^1/_2$ cup all-purpose flour, seasoned with salt and pepper

6 ounces calamari, cleaned (see page 219)

8 ounces jumbo shrimp, shelled and deveined (see page 219), plus 6 scampi or jumbo shrimp, in shells with heads

1 pound black mussels, scrubbed and debearded if necessary (see page 220)

1 pound Manila clams, scrubbed

Splash of dry sherry

6 large croutons, fried in olive oil until golden brown

To make the picada, pound the ingredients together in a mortar to make a fine paste. Set aside.

Heat $1/4$ cup of the olive oil in a large heavy pot over medium-low heat and sauté the leek until limp, 6 to 7 minutes. Add the garlic, carrot, celery, and bay leaves and cook, stirring occasionally, until the vegetables are tender, 8 to 10 minutes. Season with salt and pepper. Stir in the tomatoes and simmer for 3 to 4 minutes.

Meanwhile, heat $1/4$ cup of the olive oil in a large heavy sauté pan over medium heat and sauté the crayfish until they begin to turn pink, 3 to 4 minutes. Increase the heat to high and add $1/4$ cup of the brandy. Using a long-handled match, carefully ignite the brandy and shake the pan until the flames subside. Add the crayfish and any pan juices to the tomato mixture. Add the stock, partially cover, and simmer for 15 minutes. Pour about one-quarter of the sauce into a blender and blend until smooth. Repeat until all of the sauce has been blended. Strain the sauce through a fine-meshed sieve. Taste and correct the seasoning. Set aside.

Heat the remaining $1/4$ cup olive oil in the same sauté pan over medium-low heat. Dredge the fish fillets in the seasoned flour and sauté for 3 minutes on each side, or until lightly browned. Add the calamari, shrimp, mussels, and clams, and increase the heat to high. Add the remaining brandy. Using a long-handled match, carefully ignite the brandy and shake the pan until the flames subside. Add the sauce and picada. Cover and simmer for 5 minutes. Add the sherry and ladle into large shallow soup bowls. Serve immediately with toasted croutons on the side.

SERVES 6

Fideua de Pescado y Marisco
(Noodle and Seafood Paella)

In northeastern Spain, there are dozens of versions of this Catalan pasta dish. Some are simply short pieces of pasta fried until golden brown, simmered in fish stock, and topped with a garlicky alioli. Others, such as this one, are as elaborate as a traditional paella made with rice. Cuttlefish can be difficult to find in the United States because they are not fished in our waters but must be imported from Europe. You can use squid in their place and no one but a dedicated cuttlefish enthusiast will be able to tell the difference.

To Drink

Anchor Steam beer, dry sherry
Zarzuela recommends: Viña Sol,
Villafrance del Penedes, Spain

8 tablespoons olive oil

1 chopped onion

3 cloves garlic, minced

4 ripe tomatoes, skinned, seeded, and diced (see page 218)

8 cups Fish Fumet (page 207) or clam juice

Pinch of saffron threads

1 green bell pepper, seeded, deribbed, and diced

1 pound vermicelli or spaghetti, cut into 1-inch pieces

1 1/2 pounds monkfish, grouper, or other firm-fleshed fish fillets, cut into chunks

8 ounces cuttlefish, cut into strips, or squid cut into rings

8 ounces jumbo shrimp, shelled and deveined (see page 219), plus 6 scampi or jumbo shrimp in their shells

1 pound Manila clams, scrubbed

Kosher salt and freshly ground pepper to taste

Aioli (page 211)

Heat 2 to 3 tablespoons of the olive oil in a soup pot over medium-low heat, add the onion, and cook until very tender, about 12 minutes. Add the garlic and sauté 2 minutes more. Stir in the tomatoes and cook until the mixture is thick and concentrated, like marmalade. Add the fish fumet, increase the heat to medium-high, and bring to a boil. Skim off any foam that forms. Add the saffron, remove from the heat, and set aside.

Preheat the oven to 450°. Heat the remaining 5 to 6 tablespoons olive oil in a 16- or 18-inch paella pan over medium heat. Add the bell pepper and vermicelli, reduce the heat to low, and sauté, shaking the pan constantly, until the pasta is evenly browned, 5 to 6 minutes. Add the saffron- and vegetable-infused stock while continuing to shake the pan, and bring the liquid to a boil. Add the fish, cuttlefish, shrimp, and clams. Season with salt and pepper. Bake until all of the liquid is absorbed and the pasta is al dente, 10 to 12 minutes. Discard any clams that did not open, and serve the fideua immediately with the aioli on the side.

SERVES 6

Fish Markets of Chinatown

Although most ethnic neighborhoods of San Francisco evolve constantly, fixed in time and demographics only in a photograph, Chinatown remains a world unto itself, slow to change. As you walk up Stockton Street from Washington Square Park in the heart of North Beach, still a predominantly Italian parish, everything changes when you cross Columbus Avenue. Continue walking, and you are soon in one of the most densely populated areas of the city, the streets jammed primarily with people who live nearby, doing their day-to-day shopping. Produce stalls feature common and unfamiliar vegetables and fruits, including the infamous durian. Grocery stores display stall after stall of ingredients unrecognizable to the untrained Western eye. Signs, written in Chinese characters, offer no help. Every store has countless bins of dried sea creatures, from tiny fish not much bigger than a straight pin, minuscule shrimp, and flat, pointy-nosed fish that resemble cartoon drawings to sea cucumbers, eels, and dozens of silvery, gray, gold, and black morsels that you need a guide to identify. Some markets offer a bounty of frozen fish, eels, huge squid, whole fish, fillets, shrimp, and snails.

Continue walking until you cross Broadway, where you'll find several fresh seafood markets. You'll see enormous live geoduck clams, their shells several inches across and their bodies extended outward like thick hoses twice the length of the shells. You'll see live fish in tanks and in small Styrofoam containers with a little water; you'll also find them piled in baskets and on ice, still twitching and gasping in the air. Blue crab from Louisiana, tanks of live Dungeness crab from the Pacific, graceful spot prawns, and dozens of other species await their fate. There are huge frogs, sold live, and bins of turtles that I turn away from, acknowledging a personal boundary that I am reluctant to cross. There are familiar salmon, trout, sand dabs, rockfish, sardines, pomfret, live conch, oysters, clams, cockles, and dozens of things I couldn't identify by name if I tried. When you select a fish to take home, the fishmonger will weigh it, gut and clean it, and present it to you ready for the skillet or the roasting pan. Hurry home and cook it, before its firm sweetness deteriorates. You'll find more seafood markets one street over, on Grant Avenue, the part of Chinatown that draws the most tourists. There are also a number of Asian seafood markets on Clement Street, Irving Street, and here and there throughout the city, but not with the concentration, diversity, and intensity of the colorful Chinatown scene.

Pulpo à la Gallega (Octopus Galician Style)

One of the most popular tapas at Zarzuela is this tender, briny octopus seasoned with crunchy sea salt and good olive oil. Lucas, the chef and owner, recommends using octopus that has been frozen and thawed. Otherwise, he explains, the tentacles will be very tough and rubbery.

To Drink

Dry sherry

Zarzuela recommends: Gonzales Byass Tio Pepe

1 onion, quartered

2 tablespoons coarse sea salt, plus more for sprinkling

4 pounds octopus

1 pound new potatoes, boiled, peeled, and sliced $1/4$ inch thick

1 tablespoon Spanish paprika

Best quality extra virgin olive oil for drizzling

Bring 2 large pots of water to a boil over high heat. Add the onion and 1 tablespoon of the salt to one of the pots. Put the octopus in a colander and rinse it thoroughly under cold water, then drain. Quickly submerge the octopus in the unsalted boiling water and remove it immediately using long tongs. Repeat this step, leaving the octopus in the water for 5 seconds before lifting it out. Repeat one more time, lift the octopus out, and submerge it in the salted water. Simmer the octopus until it is tender when pierced with a wooden skewer, about 1 hour.

To serve, arrange the potatoes on individual plates. Using kitchen shears or a knife, cut the octopus tentacles into $1/8$-inch rounds and arrange several slices on top of the potatoes. Dust each portion with a little paprika, sprinkle with coarse salt, and drizzle with olive oil. Serve immediately.

SERVES 6 TO 8

Basic Recipes

Clarified Butter

When butter is melted, milk solids sink to the bottom and impurities rise to the surface. The remaining liquid is pure fat, which can be heated to higher temperatures than regular butter.

1 pound (2 cups) unsalted butter

Heat the butter in a medium saucepan over low heat until it is melted. Skim off and discard the foam and other impurities from the top of the melted butter. Carefully pour the butter into a medium container, being careful to leave the milk solids in the bottom of the pan. (It might be necessary to spoon off the final bit of melted butter rather than pour it.) Refrigerate in an airtight container for several weeks.

Brown Butter: Heat clarified butter in a saucepan over low heat until it just begins to brown and develops a nutty aroma. Remove from heat immediately. Store in an airtight container in the refrigerator for several weeks.

MAKES ABOUT $1\frac{1}{2}$ CUPS

Simple Syrup

2 cups sugar
1 cup water

Combine the sugar and water in a heavy saucepan. Do not stir. Bring to a boil over high heat, reduce heat to medium-low, and simmer for 3 to 4 minutes, or until the sugar is completely dissolved and the syrup is transparent. Remove from heat, cover, and let cool. Store in an airtight container in the refrigerator indefinitely.

MAKES ABOUT $2\frac{1}{2}$ CUPS

Tomato Concassée

2 pounds vine-ripened red tomatoes (not plum tomatoes), peeled and seeded (see page 218)
Kosher salt to taste

Using a very sharp knife, chop the tomatoes until they are almost but not quite reduced to a purée. Transfer to a medium bowl and season with salt. Use immediately, or store in an airtight container in the refrigerator for up to 2 days.

MAKES ABOUT 3 CUPS

Artichoke Hearts

2 tablespoons kosher salt
4 medium to large artichokes
About 2 teaspoons olive oil

Fill a large pot two-thirds full with water, add the salt, and boil over high heat.

Place an artichoke on your work surface, holding it on its side. Using a very sharp knife, cut off the top $1/2$ inch of the artichoke. Trim the stem end so that it is nearly flush with the bottom. Drizzle a little olive oil into the center of each artichoke and plunge them into the water, where they will float. Cook the artichokes, turning them now and then, until a leaf pulls out easily, 20 to 40 minutes, depending on the variety, size, and age of the artichokes. Drain the artichokes and let cool to the touch.

To trim the artichoke hearts, pull off all of the leaves and reserve them for another use. Use a sharp paring knife to cut out the choke in the center of each heart and trim away any pieces of leaves that cling to the heart. Use a tablespoon to scrape away any fibers of choke that remain in the center of the hearts. Cut the hearts into thin crosswise slices or leave whole, as directed in the recipe.

MAKES 4 WHOLE HEARTS OR ABOUT 1 CUP SLICED HEARTS

Vegetable Stock

You can use this flavorful, deeply colored stock in place of any poultry or meat stock. You will not, of course, achieve identical results, but it will be good.

3 unpeeled large yellow onions, quartered

Inner leaves and inner stalks of 1 head celery

3 tomatoes

1 garlic bulb, halved

6 stalks Swiss chard

2 large leeks, white parts only, halved and thoroughly rinsed

2 carrots, coarsely chopped

2 zucchini, cut into chunks

10 sprigs flat-leaf parsley

3 sprigs thyme

3 sprigs oregano

$1/_4$ cup olive oil

Preheat the oven to 325°. Put the vegetables in a large roasting pan. Sprinkle with the herbs and drizzle with the olive oil. Toss gently and roast for 30 minutes. Transfer the vegetables and pan drippings to a large stockpot, add water to cover, and simmer for $1\,1/_2$ hours, adding more water as necessary. Strain the stock, return to a clean saucepan over medium heat, and cook until reduced by one-third. Store in the refrigerator for up to 3 days, or freeze for up to 2 months.

MAKES ABOUT 4 CUPS

Light Chicken Broth

Unlike chicken stock, chicken broth is made with a greater percentage of meat than bones. It is lighter than stock, as it contains less gelatin. Broth is also not cooked as long as stock, and the chicken will retain enough flavor that it can be eaten after it is cooked. Add the ginger slices when the broth is to be used in an Asian recipe.

$1/_3$ cup kosher salt, plus more to taste
1 whole chicken, rinsed
12 cups water
1 onion, quartered
6 cloves garlic, smashed
10 sprigs flat-leaf parsley
Four $1/_4$-inch-thick ginger slices (optional)
2 teaspoons peppercorns

Fill a large pot two-thirds full with water, add the $1/_3$ cup kosher salt, and stir until it is dissolved. Add the chicken and let sit for 45 minutes. Drain thoroughly. Put the brined chicken in a large soup pot and add the water, onion, garlic, parsley, optional ginger, and peppercorns. Bring to a boil over high heat, reduce heat to medium low, cover, and simmer gently until the chicken is falling off the bone, about 2 hours.

Carefully remove the chicken from the pot. Strain the broth into a clean container and discard the vegetables and aromatics. Let the broth cool to room temperature. Refrigerate for several hours or overnight. Remove and discard the congealed fat. Store in the refrigerator for up to 3 days, or freeze for up to 3 months.

MAKES 3 QUARTS

Strong Chicken Broth: After straining the broth, pour it into a clean saucepan and bring it to a boil over medium heat. Simmer the broth until it is reduced by about one-third. Let cool, refrigerate, and remove the congealed fat before using. Makes about 9 cups.

Chicken Stock

Do not make stock with just chicken bones, or you will end up with a gelatinous and flavorless liquid. A stock needs both meat for flavor and bones for structure.

- **4 pounds chicken backs, necks, and meaty carcasses**
- **1 yellow onion, quartered**
- **1 carrot, cut into chunks**
- **1 leek, white part only, cut into chunks**
- **1 inner stalk celery, cut into chunks**
- **2 tablespoons olive oil**
- **Kosher salt to taste**
- **4 sprigs flat-leaf parsley**
- **1 teaspoon peppercorns**

Preheat the oven to 375°. Put the chicken parts, onion, carrot, leek, and celery on a rimmed baking sheet or a roasting pan and drizzle with the olive oil. Toss lightly, season with salt, and roast until lightly browned, 35 to 40 minutes.

Put the roasted chicken and vegetables, parsley, and peppercorns in a large stockpot. Add water to cover and bring to a boil over high heat. Skim off any foam that forms on top. Reduce heat and simmer for 3 to 4 hours, or until the stock is rich and concentrated. Let cool and strain. Cover and refrigerate overnight. Remove and discard the congealed fat. Store in the refrigerator for up to 3 days, or freeze for up to 3 months.

MAKES ABOUT 8 CUPS

Strong Stock

Strong, or "superior," stock, is an all-purpose stock used in both Chinese homes and restaurant kitchens. It is the ingredient that makes so many Asian soups and sauces richly flavorful. Restaurant kitchens often simmer strong stock for 10 or 20 hours, and longer. Soaking the meat in a brine solution removes blood and other impurities.

2 pounds pork ribs or necks
2 pounds pork butt or shoulder, trimmed of fat and cut into large chunks
3 pounds chicken, cut into large pieces
3 tablespoons kosher salt
2 tablespoons peanut oil or olive oil
2 shallots, thinly sliced
1 leek, white part only, thinly sliced
1 bunch green onions, trimmed and chopped
1 ham hock
1 gingerroot (about 3 ounces), crushed
2 teaspoons white peppercorns

Put the pork, chicken, and kosher salt in a large stockpot, add water to cover, and let sit for 30 minutes.

Meanwhile, heat the oil in a wok or medium sauté pan over medium heat. Add the shallots, leeks, and scallions and cook, stirring frequently, until limp, about 7 minutes.

Drain the pork and chicken, rinse the pot, and return the pork and chicken to the pot. Add the cooked vegetables, ham hock, ginger, and peppercorns. Add water to cover and bring to a boil over high heat. Skim off any foam that forms on top and reduce heat to low. Simmer for 4 to 5 hours, adding water as necessary to keep all the ingredients covered, until the stock is rich and concentrated. Let cool and strain. Cover and refrigerate overnight. Remove and discard the congealed fat. Refrigerate for up to 3 days or freeze for up to 3 months.

MAKES ABOUT 12 CUPS

Fish Fumet

Always use lean, white-fleshed fish to make fish fumet, and avoid strongly flavored fish such as mackerel and skate.

  2 1/2 to 3 pounds fish heads, tails, and bones
  2 tablespoons kosher salt
  1 yellow onion, quartered
  1 leek, white part only, quartered lengthwise
  2 small inner stalks celery, quartered
  1 teaspoon whole peppercorns
  1 bay leaf
  4 sprigs flat-leaf parsley
  3 sprigs thyme
  1 sprig oregano
  1 cup dry white wine
  8 cups water

Rinse the fish parts in cold water, removing and discarding any blood or bits of innards. Put the fish and salt in a large bowl, add water to cover, and let soak 30 minutes. Drain. Break any large fish frames into large pieces.

Put all the fish parts in a stockpot. Add the onion, leek, celery, peppercorns, and bay leaf. Use a piece of cotton twine to tie together the parsley, thyme, and oregano sprigs. Add this herb bouquet to the pot. Pour the wine and water into the pot and bring it to a boil over medium-high heat. Reduce heat to low and simmer gently for 30 minutes. Strain the mixture and discard the fish, vegetables, and herbs. Let cool to room temperature. Cover and refrigerate overnight.

Remove and discard any congealed fat. Store in the refrigerator for up to 2 days or freeze for up to 2 months.

Variation: For a stronger stock, pour the hot fumet into a clean saucepan and simmer over medium heat until reduced by half, about 15 minutes.

MAKES ABOUT 6 CUPS

Shellfish Stock

Freeze shellfish shells until you have enough to make stock.

> **2 tablespoons olive oil**
> **Shells from 2 pounds lobster, crab, or shrimp, rinsed and chopped**
> **2 cups water**
> **6 cups Fish Fumet (page 207)**

Heat the olive oil in a stockpot over medium heat, add the shellfish shells, and cook, stirring constantly, for 5 minutes. Add the water and cook until the water is nearly evaporated, 6 to 7 minutes. Add the fish fumet and bring to a boil over medium heat. Reduce heat to low and simmer for 10 minutes. Strain the stock and discard the shells. Let cool to room temperature, skim the fat from the surface, and pour the stock into a clean container, leaving any sediment in the pot. Store in the refrigerator for up to 2 days or freeze for up to 2 months.

MAKES ABOUT 6 CUPS

Seafood Velouté

Velouté is one of the classic "mother" sauces of French cuisine. It can be made with fish fumet, chicken, veal, or beef stock, and is characterized by its velvety texture.

> **3 tablespoons unsalted butter**
> **3 tablespoons all-purpose flour**
> **2 cups Fish Fumet (page 207) or Shellfish Stock (above)**
> **Salt and freshly ground pepper to taste**

Melt the butter in a medium saucepan over medium heat. Using a wooden spoon, stir in the flour and cook, stirring constantly, for 6 or 7 minutes, or until the mixture has thickened and is just barely beginning to color. Reduce heat to low. Gradually whisk in the fumet. Simmer slowly for 30 minutes, skimming off any impurities that rise to the surface. Remove from heat and season with salt and pepper. Store in the refrigerator for 2 to 3 days or freeze for up to 1 month.

MAKES ABOUT 2 CUPS

Veal Stock

Veal stock is considered a "universal stock," which means that it can be used with a variety of seafood, poultry, and meats. It is one of the essential building blocks of classic French cuisine. I recommend making veal stock several times a year and freezing it in 1-cup portions. Having veal stock on hand allows you to prepare soups, sauces, stews, and risottos quickly and easily.

4 pounds veal breast, veal trimmings, and meaty bones
Kosher salt to taste, plus 1 tablespoon
3 leeks, white part only, cut in half lengthwise
2 yellow onions, quartered
2 carrots, coarsely chopped
2 small inner stalks celery with leaves, coarsely chopped
1 tomato
3 tablespoons olive oil
$1^1/_2$ cups dry white wine
6 to 7 sprigs parsley
3 to 4 sprigs thyme
1 sprig oregano
1 bay leaf
2 teaspoons peppercorns

Preheat the oven to 375°. Cut the meat into medium-sized pieces and spread it over a roasting pan in a single layer; use 2 pans if necessary. Season with salt and roast until the meat and juices are golden brown, about 45 minutes. Spread the vegetables on a baking sheet and drizzle the olive oil over them. Toss the vegetables gently to coat them with the oil, and season them with salt to taste. Roast in the oven with the meat for 30 minutes.

Put the roasted meat and vegetables in a large stockpot. Spoon off and discard any fat in the meat-roasting pan and place the pan over medium heat. Add the white wine and stir to scrape up the browned bits from the bottom of the pan. Pour the wine and pan drippings over the meat and vegetables.

Add water to cover the meat and vegetables by 2 inches. Using cotton twine, tie together the parsley, thyme, and oregano sprigs. Add the herb bouquet to the pot. Add the bay leaf, peppercorns, and 1 tablespoon salt.

Bring to a boil over high heat, reduce heat to a simmer, partially cover, and cook until the stock is rich and flavorful, 4 to 6 hours. Add water as needed during this time to keep the meat covered. As the stock cooks, the ingredients will collapse, so you will not need as much water as you did when cooking began.

After 4 hours, taste the stock and continue cooking until the flavors are intense and concentrated. Remove from heat, strain, and let cool to room temperature. Refrigerate the stock overnight and skim off any fat that has settled on the surface. Store in the refrigerator for up to 3 days, or freeze for up to 3 months.

Beef Stock: In place of the veal, use 2 pounds lean beef, trimmed of fat and cut into chunks, and 2 to 3 pounds beef marrow bones. Roast in the oven for 30 minutes and cook as directed above.

MAKES ABOUT 12 CUPS

About Veal Demi-Glace: One of the most significant differences between a home kitchen and a restaurant kitchen is the availability of the classic mother stocks and sauces. When you're at home and a recipe calls for, say, $1/4$ cup veal demi-glace, you face 2 days of cooking to get it, unless you've wisely stored both veal stock and sauce espagnole in your freezer. In a restaurant, you simply go to the walk-in refrigerator and look for the container of demi-glace.

Sauce espagnole is one of the signature ingredients of traditional French cooking. Veal stock, wine, a roux of clarified butter and flour, and a mirepoix (minced carrots and onions) are simmered for several hours, cooled, strained and defatted, and simmered again with tomato paste and Madeira. The sauce becomes fairly thick, deeply colored, and very flavorful. To make demi-glace, equal amounts of sauce espagnole and veal stock are simmered together until the mixture is reduced by half.

There is an easier way. Many specialty markets sell frozen veal stock these days. It's not as flavorful as stock you'd make at home, but you can intensify its taste by reducing it slightly and seasoning it with salt and pepper. Even better, More Than Gourmet, a company in Akron, Ohio, makes traditional demi-glace as well as a number of concentrated stocks, including vegetable, chicken, and duck in sizes ideal for the home cook. If you cannot find these products in a store near you, call the company at 800-860-9385.

Aioli

....

The best aioli is made by hand in a mortar. It is not difficult to do; it simply takes a little time and a bit of practice. There are plenty of recipes for making aioli in a blender, but they lack the voluptuous texture and intense flavors of the handmade version because of the air incorporated into the sauce by the rapid mixing. This recipe is for classic Provençal aioli, and it packs a wallop of heat from the garlic. Some American chefs make very mild versions, using just 2 or 3 garlic cloves. Others add Dijon mustard, an ingredient found in traditional mayonnaise but not classic aioli. Feel free to adjust the ingredients to suit your taste preferences.

> 8 to 10 cloves garlic
> Pinch of kosher salt, plus salt to taste
> 1 extra-large egg yolk
> $1/2$ cup olive oil
> $1/4$ to $1/2$ cup extra virgin olive oil
> Freshly ground white pepper to taste
> 1 to 2 teaspoons hot water (optional)
> Juice of $1/2$ lemon (optional)

Put the garlic cloves in a mortar and use a wooden pestle to crush them. Sprinkle the garlic with a pinch of salt and grind the garlic cloves, crushing them against the mortar to break up the larger pieces, until they are nearly liquefied. Add the egg yolk and mix it with the garlic until a thick paste is formed. Begin to add the $1/2$ cup olive oil a few drops at a time, mixing thoroughly—with the pestle or a narrow whisk— after each addition and continuing until all of the oil has been added. Gradually mix in the extra virgin olive oil, 1 teaspoon or so at a time, until the mixture is thick and fairly stiff. Add salt and pepper to taste, and if the sauce seems too thick, mix in the hot water to thin it just slightly. Taste it again and, if you notice any bitterness, add a few drops of lemon juice and mix thoroughly. Taste again and add a little more lemon juice if the sauce needs further correcting. Cover the bowl and refrigerate for at least 30 minutes before using. Aioli will keep for 2 to 3 days, but is at its best the day it is made.

MAKES ABOUT 1 CUP

Roasted Garlic Purée

When garlic is cooked, the characteristic heat of raw garlic dissipates and the flavor becomes rich and nutty. Roasted garlic, served with croutons and goat cheese, is a popular appetizer; mashed into purée, it is an excellent addition to soups, sauces, and polenta.

> 2 garlic bulbs
> $1/2$ to $3/4$ cup olive oil
> 2 sprigs thyme
> $1/4$ cup water
> Kosher salt and freshly ground black pepper to taste

Preheat the oven to 325°. Use your fingers to peel away any loose skin on the garlic. Trim away any long roots and brush off any dirt that clings to the root end. Put the garlic bulbs in a small ovenproof saucepan or baking dish and pour about $1/2$ inch olive oil into the pan, drizzling it over the garlic as you pour. Add the thyme sprigs and water. Season with salt and pepper and cover the pan tightly with a lid or aluminum foil. Bake until the garlic is the consistency of soft butter, 45 to 60 minutes, depending on the age of the garlic. Remove from the oven and let cool to the touch.

To make the purée: Carefully break each bulb of roasted garlic into sections. Remove and discard the central stem and root. Put a section of cloves on a work surface and use the heel of one hand to press the garlic out the root end of each clove. Discard the skins, and continue until you've squeezed out all of the garlic. Mash the garlic with a fork and put it in a small bowl. Set aside for up to 1 hour, or cover and refrigerate for up to 3 days.

MAKES 4 TO 6 TABLESPOONS

Creamy Polenta

The secret to making good polenta is to use coarse-ground cornmeal that has not gone rancid (cornmeal should always be stored in the refrigerator), cook it in enough water, and cook it long enough for the individual grains of corn to become tender. Do not use instant polenta, which has an insipid texture.

> 6 cups water
> 2 teaspoons kosher salt, plus salt to taste
> 1 cup coarse-ground polenta
> 4 cloves garlic, pressed
> 2 tablespoons unsalted butter
> $1/_2$ cup grated dry jack or Parmigiano-Reggiano cheese
> Freshly ground pepper to taste

Pour 3 cups of the water into a medium saucepan, add the 2 teaspoons salt, and bring to a boil over high heat. Pour the remaining 3 cups of water into another small saucepan and place it over medium-low heat to maintain at a simmer. Using a whisk, stir the boiling water rapidly in a circular direction to create a vortex and pour the polenta into the vortex in a thin, steady stream, whisking constantly. Decrease heat to medium-low and continue to whisk as the polenta thickens. Replace the whisk with a wooden spoon, stir in 1 cup of the simmering water, and continue to stir. If you find any lumps, use the back of the wooden spoon to press them against the side of the saucepan.

Continue to stir the polenta until it is very thick and pulls away from the side of the saucepan. Taste it occasionally and add more of the simmering water if it becomes too thick before the grains of corn are tender. It will take 20 to 60 minutes for the polenta to cook, depending on the age of the corn and size of the grains. When the polenta is tender, add the garlic, butter, and cheese and stir thoroughly. Correct the seasoning with salt and pepper to taste. Serve immediately, or cover and hold over simmering water for up to 30 minutes.

SERVES 4 TO 6

Toasted Garlic Bread

There are many ways to make good garlic bread. If you use good ingredients—real butter, fresh garlic, fresh herbs—it's hard to go wrong. Some cooks insist on using unsalted butter, but I do not think it is necessary. Use whatever butter you normally use. The main reason to use unsalted butter is because it has a shorter shelf life and so may be fresher than salted butter. This is a concern only in areas without a nearby dairy industry, where butter must be shipped a great distance.

$1/_2$ cup (1 stick) butter
2 to 6 cloves garlic, minced
1 tablespoon minced fresh flat-leaf parsley leaves
1 teaspoon minced fresh thyme
1 teaspoon minced fresh oregano
One 1-pound loaf San Francisco—style sourdough bread
Chunk of Parmigiano-Reggiano cheese (optional)

Preheat the oven to 375°. Melt the butter in a small saucepan over medium-low heat. Add the garlic and cook for 30 seconds. Stir in the parsley, thyme, and oregano and remove from heat.

Cut the loaf of bread in half lengthwise. Using a pastry brush, cover the cut surface of both pieces of bread with the garlic butter and herbs. Use all of the butter, and be sure to scoop up the pieces of garlic and press them into the bread. Grate cheese, if using, over the entire surface of the bread. Place the bread on a baking sheet and bake until heated through and lightly browned on top, 10 to 12 minutes. Cut into 2-inch-wide wedges and serve immediately.

SERVES 4 TO 6

Preserved Lemons

When lemons soak in salt and their own juices, their skins soften and become entirely edible. Preserved lemons have been used as a condiment in North African cuisines for centuries, and have become increasingly popular in the United States in the last decade. Although there are a few commercial brands available, those are preserved in vinegar brines and have a much different taste and texture than those you make at home.

> **5 lemons**
> **$1/_4$ cup kosher salt**
> **1 tablespoon sugar**
> **1 cup freshly squeezed lemon juice (4 to 5 lemons)**

Put the lemons in a deep, narrow bowl and pour boiling water to cover them. Soak for 15 minutes and drain. Repeat twice. Let cool.

Using a sharp knife, cut each lemon into 6 to 8 lengthwise wedges. Carefully remove any exposed seeds. In a medium bowl, toss together the lemon wedges, salt, and sugar. Pack the lemons and all of the salt into a glass pint jar and pour in the lemon juice. Press the lemons down so that they are completely covered by the lemon juice. Cover the jar opening with plastic wrap and close the jar tightly with its lid.

Place the jar on a saucer and store it in a cool, dark cupboard for 5 days. Twice each day, shake the jar to help the lemons age evenly. If the lemons are not completely submerged in the juice, turn the jar upside down in the morning; at night, turn it upright. As the lemons soften, they will collapse into the liquid. After 5 days, the lemons should be tender and ready for use. If they still seem a little tough, age for 2 more days. Store in the refrigerator for 6 to 8 weeks.

MAKES 2 CUPS

Basic Techniques

Preparing an Ice-Water Bath: Fill a medium or large bowl about one-third full with ice and cover the ice with water, making sure the bowl is no more than half full. To shock, or refresh, vegetables, (a process that stops cooking and sets color), plunge them into the bath for a minute or two, then drain them thoroughly. To shock seafood such as crab, immerse it in the ice water for several minutes, or until cool. To use the bath when making a sauce, put a pan or bowl directly into the ice water.

Reducing a Liquid: Reducing a liquid simply means to evaporate it over heat. Wine, water, and stock should be simmered over medium heat until reduced by the percentage called for in a specific recipe. To reduce milk, half-and-half, or cream, you'll need to use a large saucepan, because the liquid will increase in volume as it heats. If the pot is too small, the liquid will boil over.

Skinning Hazelnuts: Hazelnuts and many other nuts need to have their thin inner skins removed before they are used in certain recipes. To remove the skins by blanching, place the nuts in a bowl, cover them with boiling water, and agitate the bowl for several seconds. Let sit for 45 seconds, then drain. Add water to cover and let sit for 30 minutes. Drain well. Dry the nuts on a tea towel and rub them between two tea towels to remove the skins. To remove the skins by toasting the nuts, a technique that intensifies their flavor, follow the technique described in Toasting Nuts, Seeds, and Spices. After the nuts are toasted, rub them between the folds of a tea towel to loosen their skins.

Toasting Nuts, Seeds, and Spices: Toasting nuts, seeds, and spices alters their flavors in subtle ways. Walnuts, for example, contain harsh tannins that are softened when they are toasted. Heat intensifies the flavors and aromas of many spices, such as cumin seeds. Toast in a heavy sauté pan over medium heat. Use a pan that holds the food to be toasted in a single layer, and add the nuts, seeds, or spices to the pan before placing it over heat. Place over medium heat and agitate the pan constantly so that the nuts, seeds, or spices do not burn. Toast spices until they are fragrant, and toast nuts until they just begin to color. Transfer to a plate or bowl immediately. If left in the hot pan, the food will continue to cook and may burn.

Making Fresh Bread Crumbs: Fresh bread crumbs are made with 1- to 2-day-old bread. For the smoothest crumbs, remove all crusts, cut the bread first into slices and then into chunks, and put a handful of chunks in a blender or food processor. Pulse until the bread is reduced to an even crumb. For coarser crumbs, leave the crusts on the bread. If the bread is very fresh, it is difficult to make crumbs. You will need to slice the bread, cut it into chunks, and let it dry for 1 day. Alternatively, spread the cubes in a single layer on a rimmed baking sheet and dry in a preheated 250° oven for about 40 minutes.

Toasting Fresh Bread Crumbs: Toast small quantities of fresh bread crumbs by heating 1 tablespoon olive oil in a heavy skillet over medium heat. Add the bread crumbs, toss gently but thoroughly, and cook, agitating the pan all the while, until the bread crumbs are golden brown, about 7 to 8 minutes.

To toast larger quantities, toss bread crumbs with 2 teaspoons olive oil per 1 cup bread crumbs and spread them out evenly in a rimmed baking sheet. Toast in a preheated 300° oven until golden brown, 10 to 12 minutes.

Making Croutons: There are two types of croutons: thin slices of baguettes or other hearth-style breads, and cubes of bread that have been toasted in an oven or fried in olive oil. In this book, sliced croutons are called for in several recipes. To make sliced croutons, cut bread into diagonal slices about $1/4$ inch wide. Brush each slice lightly with olive oil, place on a baking sheet in a single layer, and toast in a preheated 300° oven until golden brown, 15 to 20 minutes. A 1-pound baguette will make about 25 croutons.

Citrus Zest: Citrus zest is made from the thin, colored outer layer of the skin of any citrus fruit, though the most common zests are from lemons, oranges, and limes. This layer of skin contains the delicate and flavorful volatile oils of the fruit. The easiest way to make zest is by using a Microplane grater-zester, one of the finest kitchen tools to come along in decades. It is so quick and easy that you can zest a dozen lemons in the amount of time it once took to remove the zest of a single one. (You can also use these zesters for grating hard cheeses.) I consider this tool as essential as a good knife. You can find them in most cookware stores.

Alternatively, use a zester, which has a handle similar to a paring knife and a short, flat blade with several sharp holes. As you scrape the blade over the surface of the fruit, a thin julienne of zest is removed.

When neither of these tools is available, do not use a standard cheese grater or you'll likely end up with grated knuckles. Instead, use a vegetable peeler to shave off thin pieces of zest, then use a sharp knife to cut it into julienne or to mince it.

Make zest shortly before using it. If you must make it in advance, wrap it tightly in plastic wrap and store it in the refrigerator for up to 4 hours so it doesn't dry out.

Cutting Citrus Segments: To cut lemon, lime, orange, grapefruit, or pomello segments, cut off both ends of the fruit down to the flesh and set the fruit upright on a work surface. Hold the fruit steady with one hand, and with the other hand use a sharp knife to cut off the peel down to the flesh, cutting downward and following the curve of the fruit. The fruit should be completely free of white pith. Now, hold the fruit in the palm of your hand, with a bowl underneath to catch drippings. Cut close to each membrane to loosen the segments of citrus, which will gently slip out.

Shaving Vegetables: Shaved vegetables are simply vegetables so thinly sliced they are almost translucent. You need a very sharp knife and a steady hand to do this. You can also use a vegetable peeler to make very thin shavings of vegetables that are fairly large, like carrots. You can also use a mandoline, available in better cookware stores, with the blade on the narrowest setting. (A mandoline—the best cost about $150 or more—is a good investment if you do a lot of cooking.)

Sweating Vegetables: To sweat vegetables, cook them in a small amount of butter or other fat over very low heat, so that they cook as slowly as possible. This technique develops flavor gently and completely and allows natural sugars to begin to caramelize. You do not need to stir the vegetables as they sweat; if they appear to be burning, either the heat is too high or you have not used enough fat, in which case you should reduce the heat or add a small amount of butter. This is the technique that should be used when onions are cooked longer than 15 minutes.

Peeling and Seeding Tomatoes: Most cookbooks and television cooking shows tell you to peel a tomato by plunging it first into boiling water and then into ice water, but boiling water cooks too much of a tomato's flesh and any water at all dilutes its flavor. A better technique is to quickly blister the skins. To do so, turn a burner on a stove to high (gas works best, but you can use electric burners, too; just be sure they're hot before you begin). Spear a tomato through its stem end with the tines of a fork and hold the tomato close to the heat. Turn it constantly as the skin shrinks and cracks; it needn't actually blacken, though there will likely be a few darkened patches. Place the tomato in a large bowl to cool and repeat the process as necessary; each tomato should take only 12 to 15 seconds. After the tomatoes have cooled for 3 or 4 minutes, use your fingers to pull off the skins, which should come off very easily. This technique preserves a tomato's fresh flavor and texture.

To seed a tomato, use a paring knife to cut out the stem core and cut the tomato in half crosswise. Hold one half, cut-side down, in the palm of your hand and gently squeeze out the seeds and gel over a sink, using a finger of your other hand to coax them out if necessary.

Roasting and Peeling Peppers and Chiles: To roast any fresh pepper or chile, preheat a stovetop grill or start a charcoal fire in an outdoor grill. Refrigerate the peppers or chiles for at least an hour. When the grill is hot, arrange the vegetables in a single layer. Turn them frequently with tongs until their skins are evenly scorched; do not overcook them, or their flesh will be mushy. Put the scorched vegetables in a large bowl, cover it with a tea towel, and let them steam for 15 or 20 minutes.

Use your fingers to pull off the seared skins, and a paring knife to cut out the stem and seed core. (If you are working with hot chiles, such as jalapenos, wear latex gloves or scrub your hands thoroughly after preparing them so that you do not burn yourself with the chile oil.) Cover and store roasted peppers or chiles in the refrigerator for up to 3 days.

Shelling and Deveining Shrimp: Hold a single shrimp in one hand, and with the fingers of your other hand grab the legs on the curved inner side of the shrimp and pull them off. Holding the tail end, pull off the shell segments. If the recipe calls for the tail to be removed, pinch it off; otherwise, leave it in place. Use a paring knife to make a shallow slit near the head end of the outer curve of the shrimp. Pull out and discard the dark intestine that runs the length of the shrimp. Rinse, drain, and dry the shrimp after you have peeled and cleaned them.

Cleaning and Peeling Calamari: Sometimes calamari, or squid, are sold already cleaned, but it's easy enough to clean them yourself. First, cut off the tentacles as close to the eyes as possible, so that the tentacles remain intact rather than separating into individual strands. Hold the body, or mantle, in one hand and squeeze out the entrails. Reach inside the mantle and pull out the transparent quill. Squeeze the tentacles to remove the round beak nestled inside. Discard the entrails, quill, and beak and rinse the tentacles and the body inside and out. To peel the bodies, which is not necessary but is recommended by some cooks, use your fingers to pull away the thin, purplish skin that clings to the mantle.

Cleaning and Filleting Skate Wing: Skate is a member of the family of fish that includes sharks, stingrays, and gorgeous giant manta rays. There are several species in California waters. The fish have large pectoral fins that look like wings, hence their name. Skate wing is just now becoming popular in restaurants in the United States, and is still unfamiliar to most home cooks. This is unfortunate, because it is beautiful, delicious, and very inexpensive.

You will probably have to ask your fishmonger or butcher to order skate for you; ask for a wing that weighs about 1 1/2 pounds, enough to serve 4. If you need more, get 2 wings; larger wings may be tough and strongly flavored. The wing will likely arrive with the skin already removed. Each wing includes two fillets separated by a system of cartilage. To remove the fillets, use a sharp boning knife to trim away any remaining skin, fat, and exposed cartilage. Beginning near the thick center, slide the boning knife under the meat and move the blade along the skeleton until you loosen the fillet at the wing tip. Cut the fillet in half and turn the wing around to remove the other half of the fillet. Next, turn the wing over and remove the second fillet in the same fashion. Skate wing is very thin and needs only the briefest cooking.

Scrubbing and Debearding Mussels: Not so long ago, most mussels needed to be scrubbed with a hard plastic or wire brush before you cooked them. You also needed to trim off their beards with kitchen shears. This is still the case with wild mussels. Rinse wild mussels in cold water; scrub their outer shells to remove grit, barnacles, and seaweed, then trim off the dark beard that hangs out of the shells with sharp shears.

Farm-raised mussels rarely, if ever, have beards or barnacles. Rinse the mussels in cold water, discard any that don't close when touched, and shake off excess water before cooking them.

Discarding Unopened Mussels, Clams, and Oysters: Not all shellfish open identically, and you should look at them closely before discarding any because you think they are closed. Some perfectly good shellfish open just a little, while their companions fall into a gaping yawn after just a couple of minutes over heat. Look at each one to decide if it's okay. A clam, mussel, or oyster that was dead before it went into the pot will not open at all, nor will most empty shells. Be sure to remove the closed shells before you try to open them; occasionally one will be filled with mud or sand, which you do not want falling into the main dish. Look at the shell; if it has opened at all, it is likely just fine. If, however, the meat inside looks shriveled, toss it.

Buying, Cooking, Cleaning, and Cracking Dungeness Crab: You can buy cooked Dungeness crab at Fisherman's Wharf and in markets all over the Bay Area, and it is usually very good. But for the very best, you must buy it live and cook it yourself. At first, the task seems daunting, but you'll quickly get the hang of it. Begin with a crab that seems heavy for its size and is energetic and feisty. One time when I ordered crab in a restaurant, an immense chef waddled out from the kitchen, stuck long tongs into an aquarium in the dining room, and pulled out one of the biggest Dungeness crabs I've ever seen. The irascible creature fought the chef all the way to the kitchen, waving his claws menacingly in an attempt to free himself. Thirty minutes later, the crab was set before me, perfectly chilled; nothing has ever tasted better.

To cook your cranky crab, fill a large pot about half full with water and salt it heavily, about $1/4$ cup salt per gallon of water, and bring it to a boil over high heat. When it boils, quickly put the crab in the water, head down, and cover the pan. An alternate cooking method, recommended by Jay Harlow, author of *West Coast Seafood: The Complete Cookbook* (Sasquatch Books, 1999) is to put the crab in cold water and raise the temperature slowly, a technique that some scientists believe might be more humane. (Others suggest hitting the crab on the head with a hammer before cooking it, but I've never been very good at this.) Cook small crabs for about 7 minutes, larger ones for 10 to 12 minutes. Use tongs to transfer the crab to an ice-water bath (see page 217); let the crab chill in the water for about 10 minutes, then drain it thoroughly and pat it dry.

To clean the crab, hold it in one hand, top-side up, and with the other hand, grasp the top shell and lift it up, pulling it away from the body. Set the shell aside.

Turn the crab over and tug on the breastplate, a triangle-shaped section, lifting it up and off the crab. Turn the crab over again and remove and discard the finger-like gills on either side of the body. Remove and discard the intestine, nestled in the center of the back, and twist off the mouth. If the recipe you're using calls for the butter, the mustardy yellow edible organs and fat located in the body cavity, remove and reserve it. Twist off the legs and set them aside. Rinse the body under cold water to remove any remaining butter and break it in half with your hands or with a large cleaver. Pick out the body meat, being sure to remove all shells. Use a small mallet or a nutcracker to crack the legs, and use your fingers to remove the meat. To serve cracked crab, leave both the body and leg meat in their shells. To use the top shells, wash them thoroughly.

Shucking Oysters: Shucking oysters is not difficult, but it does take strength, practice, and the proper tools. You'll need an oyster knife and a heavy-duty glove of some sort; there are special oyster gloves made with woven metal threads. Scrub the oysters to remove grit, mud, or broken pieces of shell. Drain and place them in a large container. Have a bed of ice or a baking sheet at hand. Put the glove on and hold the oyster in the palm of your hand with the cup, which is the deeper half of the shell, down, and the hinge of the shell, also called the beak, pointed towards you. Fit the oyster knife in the tiny slot between the two shells and work the tip back and forth, pressing to penetrate the shell. Once the knife has been wedged into the oyster, twist it back and forth to open the shell. At this point, the muscle will still be holding the two sides of the shell together. Keeping the knife parallel, slide it across the top of the oyster to cut the abductor muscle. Remove the top shell and run the knife under the body of the oyster to loosen it, being carefully not to let the liquor run out. Discard the top shell, set the shucked oyster on ice or on the sheet pan, and continue until all of the oysters have been opened.

INDEX